History
Revision

James Fuller

Contents

Middle-aged spread

Sir Ralph Witherbottom was cross with his daughter Izzy. Some harsh words had been spoken at dinner and the atmosphere in the house was black. Spotless, the family dog, was hiding outside in his kennel. Max, the long suffering housekeeper, butler and man of many talents was upstairs trying to explain something complicated to Izzy.

'People get very sensitive about their age after a certain point in their lives, Izzy,' said Max.

'But all I asked was whether Dad had seen the church being built. He's middle aged, the church is from the Middle Ages!'

'Ohhhhh, I see. You realise, don't you, that the church is over 700 years old and that the Middle Ages is very different from being middle aged. Look at this history timeline – it might just do the trick. Timelines are used by historians to show the different parts of history.'

European History

1–600 Classical Period

600–1000 Dark Ages

1000–1450 Middle Ages

1066

1450–1789 Early Modern Period

1790 – today Modern Period

1 200 400 600 800 1000 1200 1400 1600 1800 2000

Izzy took the paper and looked for a while. She found that the Middle Ages had lasted for hundreds of years, but something bothered her.

'Where are the Tudors, then?' she asked. Izzy was about to study Tudors at school, and the Victorians, and she felt sure that these should be included.

Max explained. 'Sometimes history is divided into big sections called periods and sometimes historians divide the periods up into reigns. Here, look, this is a timeline of English history divided up by royal families.' From somewhere else in his suit, Max pulled out another timeline.

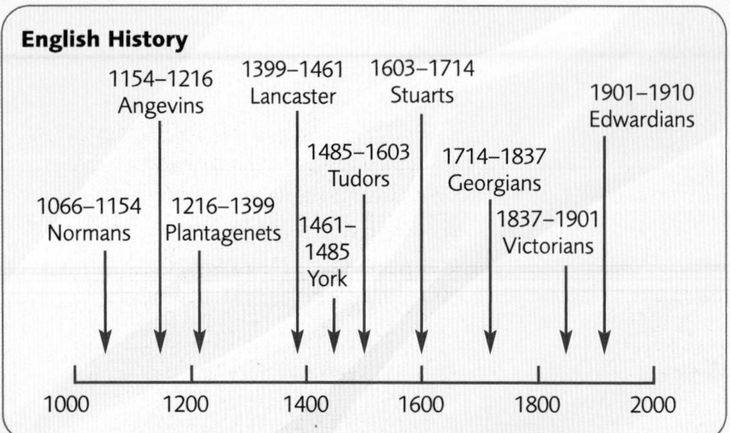

'Do you know, Max, I think I am beginning to understand. I can feel an investigation coming on. If Dad doesn't belong to the Middle Ages then what does? Can we find something out about the period?'

And so they did.

Middle English muddle

Match Chaucer's words with their modern meaning. When you have done this, take the first letter of each word and unscramble the anagram to reveal one of Chaucer's other jobs.

	Chaucer's word	Modern meaning
1	Cristen	Rust
2	Myghte	Might
3	Oxenford	Offering
4	Everich	Iron
5	Ruste	Flowers
6	Iren	Courteous
7	Flours	Understand
8	Ooffryng	Smiling
9	Frenssh	Every
10	Ttrappe	French
11	Smylying	Trap
12	Curteis	Side
13	Syde	Christian
14	Understonde	Oxford

Chaucer

Answer

....

....

• TOP TIPS •

Literature should not just be studied in English lessons. Books written in the time that is being studied can tell historians a great deal about the period.

DID YOU KNOW?

Chaucer was not just a writer, he was also a traveller, a spy and a customs officer.

Test your knowledge 4

1 Fill in the missing dates.

a) The church in Izzy's village was built in the 14th Century. This means that it was built between the years .... and ....

b) St Benedict wrote the rules for monks in AD ....

c) In which decade was Chaucer born? ....

(3 marks)

2 Fill in the gaps.

People went to church for many reasons.

a) People were scared of going to ....

b) People had no knowledge of .... and therefore no understanding of things like lightening.

c) People believed that God could have control over people's .... and therefore prayed when people were ill.

d) .... scared people with gory pictures of demons.

(4 marks)

3 Where in a church would you find the following features?

a) Belfry ....

b) Yew tree ....

c) Weather vane ....

d) Porch ....

e) Buttress ....

f) Gargoyle ....

(6 marks)

4 Answer these questions with one word or a short sentence.

a) Name the building that monks live in.

....

b) What did monks wear?

....

c) List at least five jobs that monks did.

....

....

d) What is the female equivalent of a monk?

....

e) What was a monk's haircut called?

....

(5 marks)

5 Circle the odd one out. Then give a reason why it is the odd one out.

a) A Eggs B Eggies C Epples D Eyren

....

b) A Middle English B Anglo-Saxon C Norman French D Latin

....

c) A Writing B Farming C Teaching D Eating crisps

....

d) A Tonsure B Habit C Cross D Trainers

....

(4 marks)

(Total 22 marks)

Everybody's going serfing

'What was it like to live in the Middle Ages?' Izzy had been reading a celebrity lifestyle magazine that morning and had been very impressed with what she saw. 'Any swimming pools, computer games, fast food takeaways or shopping centres?'

'Sorry, Izzy,' replied Max. 'Most people lived in tiny villages. They were peasants – just simple farmers.'

'However, it was a bit more complicated than that. Serfs had no land at all and worked for the lords. Other peasants were known as villeins and freemen and they often had some land of their own. The village was often run by a reeve, and taxes in the form of crops or sometimes money were paid to the Lord of the manor. Let's build a model.'

And so between them, Izzy and Max produced this model of a medieval village.

'Max, why have you made the fields like that?' enquired Izzy curiously. 'They look stupid.'

'Aaaah ... this is one of the most important things about the way that medieval villages worked. Because they didn't have artificial fertilisers and chemicals they couldn't put too much pressure on the fields. All the men in the village were given strips in the three fields, and everyone had to grow the same crop in each field.'

'So, for example, one year the North field would have wheat, the West field would have barley, and they would leave the East field fallow. That is when you leave it for a year to recover and the animals deposit manure on it. This whole system is called crop rotation.'

Sam's stolen stuff

• TOP TIPS •

History is often divided into different categories:

- **When it is about ordinary people and their lives it is known as <u>social history</u>.**
- **When it is about kings, governments and wars it is known as <u>political history</u>.**

Try to understand what type of history you are studying.

Samuel the peasant has gone out, and a thief has been into his house.
Circle the objects that have been stolen?

DID YOU KNOW?

Peasants were not allowed to leave the village without permission from the Lord of the manor.

Man about town

'What about the towns, Max?' said Ralph. 'I know that they were better. They had something called a charter, which gave the townspeople more rights and freedom. There was also more trade, some shops, and more entertainment for townspeople. I would have preferred to live in a town in the Middle Ages.'

'Me too,' agreed Izzy. 'Is there anything else good about towns?'

Ralph continued. 'If a villager managed to escape to a town for a year he no longer had to obey the lord of the manor of the village he came from. Also, townspeople elected their leader, the mayor, who was helped by the guilds.'

'The what?'

'Guilds, Izzy. These were trade organisations that ran each trade. Let's use shoemaking as an example.'

Max wanted his say too. 'Life in the towns wasn't all good. They were full of diseases, they had no sewage system or rubbish collectors and crime was a real problem. But you are right, Izzy, in many ways it was probably better to live in a town.'

Streetwise

Spot ten differences in the street scenes below.

DID YOU KNOW?

Hardly any of our major cities were important in the Middle Ages. Places like Birmingham, Manchester, Leeds and Sheffield all grew up in the 1800s.

• TOP TIPS •

Use the proper names for things when writing about history. A good word to use for things to do with cities and towns is <u>urban</u>.

Soup of the month

Izzy had a brainwave. She announced that they were all going to eat like medieval peasants for the day. Their 'lovely' menu is shown below.

<u>The Pleasant Peasant Menu</u>

<u>Breakfast</u>

Coarse dark bread made from barley, oats, rye or sometimes even made from acorns. Onion or salt to give it flavour.

Water or ale.

<u>Lunch</u>

Cheese, coarse bread.

Water or ale.

<u>Dinner</u>

<u>Pottage</u> made with herbs, onions, turnips and whatever else was available. (If they were lucky the peasants would sometimes be able to add a small piece of bacon or rabbit to the stew.)

Water or ale.

Ralph and Max cooperated. However, after Izzy had gone to bed Max prepared a special Lord's meal which he and Ralph ate washed down with plenty of wine.

<u>Max's Lord's menu</u>

<u>Dinner</u>

Fine white bread, stewed beef, boiled bacon, roast peacock, roast wild boar. Cakes, tarts and sweetmeats (fried animal hearts, livers etc).
Wine or ale.

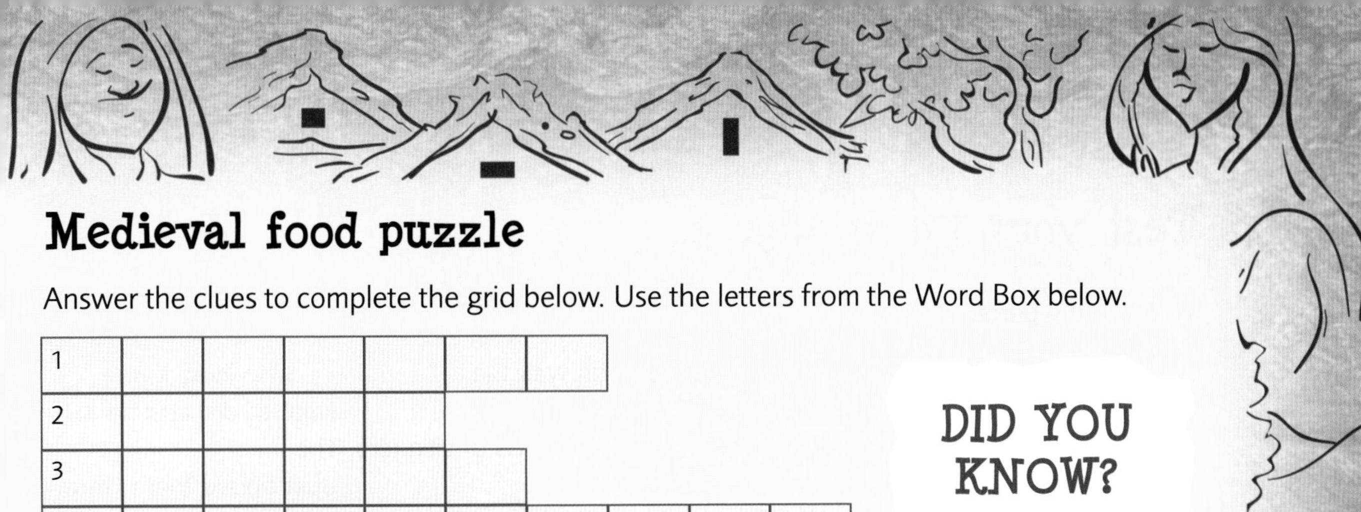

Medieval food puzzle

Answer the clues to complete the grid below. Use the letters from the Word Box below.

1									
2									
3									
4									
5									
6									
7									

1 Type of soup a peasant might eat.
2 A round fruit that can be red or green.
3 A red, peppery vegetable.
4 Name for liver, hearts, etc.
5 He gets wine to drink.
6 Time of day that the peasant had his main meal.
7 What you might say if you were forced to eat a peasant's food.

DID YOU KNOW?

Potatoes were not on the peasant's menu during the Middle Ages. It is thought that Sir Walter Ralegh may have introduced potatoes to England during the reign of Elizabeth I. They are South American.

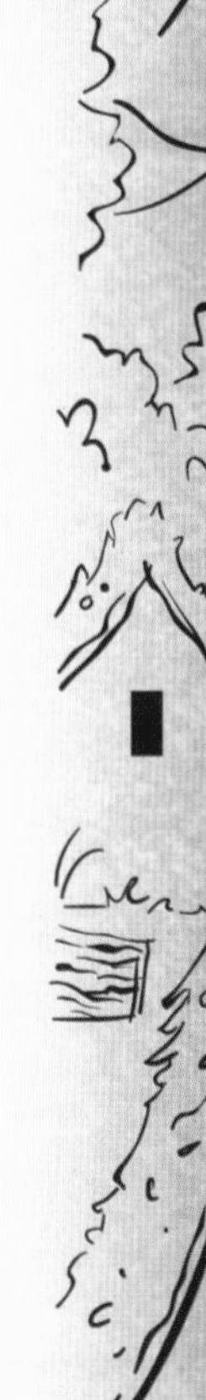

Word box

There are two hidden words in this food puzzle:

1 If you have completed the grid correctly, there is a hidden word running down the first column.
2 You have not used some of the letters in the Word Box. Unscramble the remaining letters to find the second hidden word.

(Clue: The two hidden words are connected.)

AGE	L	LE	NING
S	POTT	RAD	ERB
APP	ISH	TME	ATS
H	ORD	WEE	
EVE	Y	UCK	

Hidden words: ....

....

• TOP TIPS •

Izzy's recipe for pottage:

- **Cut up one onion and some garlic. Fry for 10 minutes.**
- **Add chopped carrot, turnip and a big handful of herbs (thyme, parsley, sage, rosemary) and perhaps some bacon. Fry for 5 more minutes.**
- **Add 1 litre of vegetable stock. Simmer for about 30 minutes.**
- **Add salt to taste.**

Please ask permission to cook this.

Test your knowledge 5

1 Fill in the gaps.

In a medieval village the most important person was the .... who lived in the manor house. His official, the steward, would tell the .... what to do, and he in turn would tell the villagers. There were different types of villagers. The .... were the lowest of the low and they often owned no .... Just above them were .... and .... These villagers are known collectively as ....

(7 marks)

2 Cross out the incorrect words to make sense out of this paragraph.

In the Middle Ages, towns usually had a *supermarket/charter*. This was *a legal document/a big wall* that outlined the town's rights. Usually *a king/a mayor* ran a town. He would usually have been *picked out of a hat/elected*. The powerful organisations within the town would have been the various *sports clubs/guilds*. These ran all of the *trades/pitches*.

A medieval town would have had lots of *rubbish/balloons* in the street. It was easy to catch *diseases/flying fish* and they were not hygienic places to live. However, a townsman would have more *freedom/pens* than a villager.

(9 marks)

3 Answer these questions with one word or a short sentence.

a) What root vegetable would a medieval peasant never have eaten?

....

b) What did a lord often drink that a peasant would not?

....

c) What was pottage?

....

d) What does the word 'coarse' mean when describing the peasant's bread?

....

e) In modern English, what word do we more usually use for ale?

....

(5 marks)

4 Circle the odd one out. Then give a reason why it is the odd one out.

a) A Ox B Pig C Turkey D Sheep

....

b) A Dishwasher B Spade C Cauldron D Scythe

....

c) A Charter B Guild C Mayor D Bowling alley

....

d) A Serf B Lord C Villein D Freeman

....

e) A Fallow B Wheat C Sweetcorn D Barley

....

(5 marks)

(Total 26 marks)

What a knightmare

'Next week I am going on a business trip to France,' announced Ralph. 'I want you to come with me, Izzy, and I can show you the site of one of the most famous battles in history – Agincourt. All part of the Hundred Years War, you know.'

<u>Rules of chivalry</u>

These are rules for knights fighting other knights. They are not for ordinary soldiers.

1 Love God.
2 Be brave and honourable at all times.
3 Honour women.
4 Don't strike an enemy when he is down.
5 Accept an enemy knight's surrender.
6 Don't lie, cheat or steal.

I hope that this 50 year war stops soon!

One week later, on a ferry...

'Did you say a war that lasted 100 years?' asked Izzy between mouthfuls of croissant. 'That's amazing.'

'Actually, the wars between Britain and France lasted longer than 100 years,' replied Ralph. 'But they didn't exactly go on continuously. It was more like a long series of wars. Most kings of England at this time thought that they should be King of France as well, especially after Edward III. The really tough ones tried to do something about it. There were three main battles, two for Edward III – Crecy in 1346, Poitiers in 1356 – and one for Henry V – Agincourt in 1415. But much of the fighting was done in smaller local battles and <u>sieges</u>.'

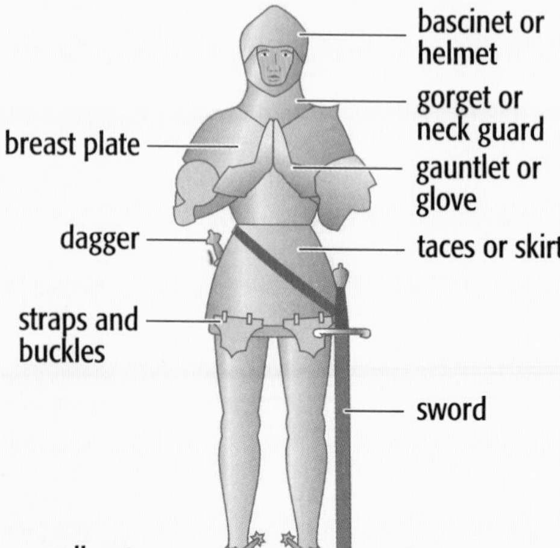
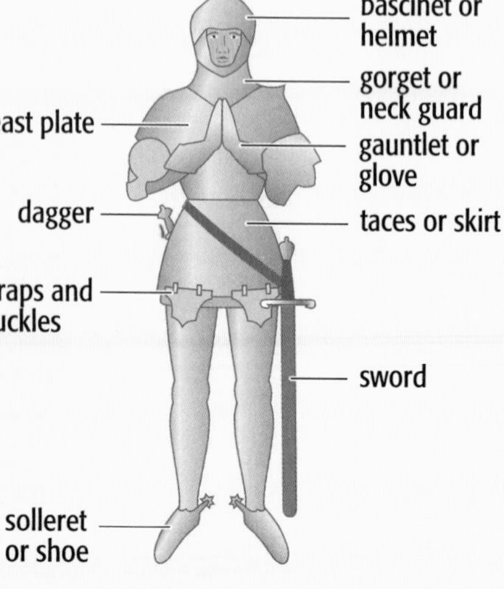

'Well I know all about battles,' said Izzy. 'I've looked at Hastings and that was between England and France. I can't possibly need to know any more?'

'No, no, no, Izzy,' Ralph argued. 'This was nearly 400 years later and things had changed. The Hundred Years War ran from about 1340 to about 1460. We are talking <u>knights</u>, <u>chivalry</u> and huge <u>suits of armour</u>. Here, look at this picture and then compare it with one of William's knights.'

The grail quest

Only one of these knights will succeed in his quest for the Holy Grail. Which one will get there, Sir Richard, Sir James, Sir Ian or Sir Neil? Circle your answers.

DID YOU KNOW?

King Arthur's Knights of the Round Table are not real historical figures. However, stories about Arthur were very popular in the Middle Ages because they were about chivalry. One of the most important parts of chivalry was having a holy quest.

Chivalry's highest honour is the Order of the Garter, invented by Edward III. Important people can still be awarded it today and there can only be 26 Knights of the Garter at any one time.

The Queen at a modern Order of the Garter ceremony

• TOP TIPS •

Image was everything to most medieval kings. Kings in the Middle Ages were always trying to prove that they were chivalrous. You can see this in paintings and writings and read about it in accounts of their wartime actions.

Badgers, badges and gules

Ralph was trying to explain heraldry to Izzy.

'Look, Izzy, there were no uniforms on a medieval battlefield. Knights had their own armour, often made by Italian armourers. It was impossible to tell who to kill and who to protect. So family coats of arms were used to show which knight was which. The knight displayed them on his horse, his coat, his banner and his shield. His servants and men sometimes wore his colours too.'

'What have arms got to do with it?' Izzy really was not in a very serious mood.

'Coats of arms ... the family badge,' replied Ralph trying to keep it serious. 'Eventually, the art of heraldry became a very important one and all important families had coats of arms.'

'Look, here is the famous Witherbottom coat of arms. Our family was awarded these in the 1400s and a Witherbottom fought in the Battle of Agincourt. A full coat of arms has lots of features from top to bottom.'

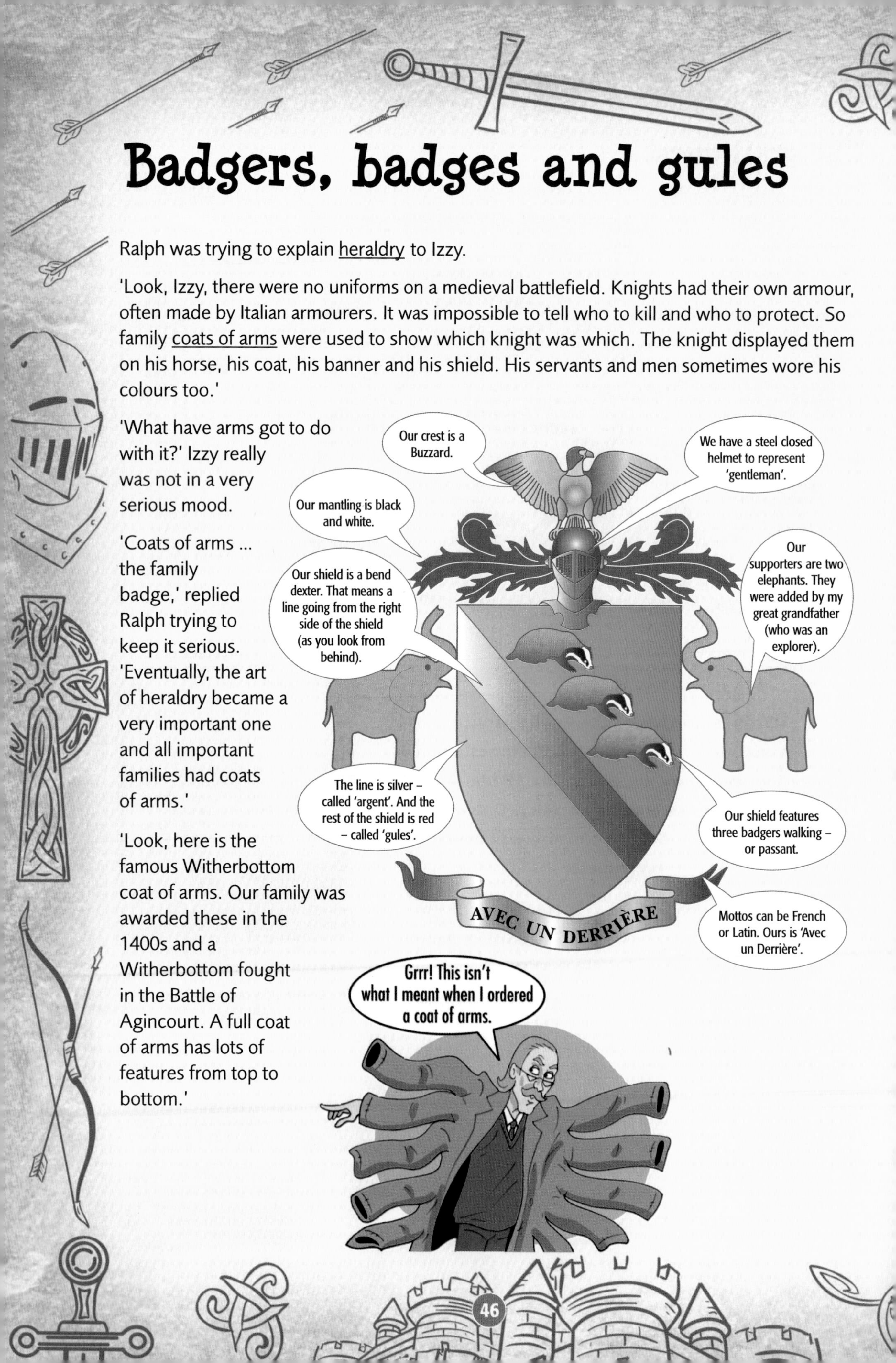

Shield mirror images

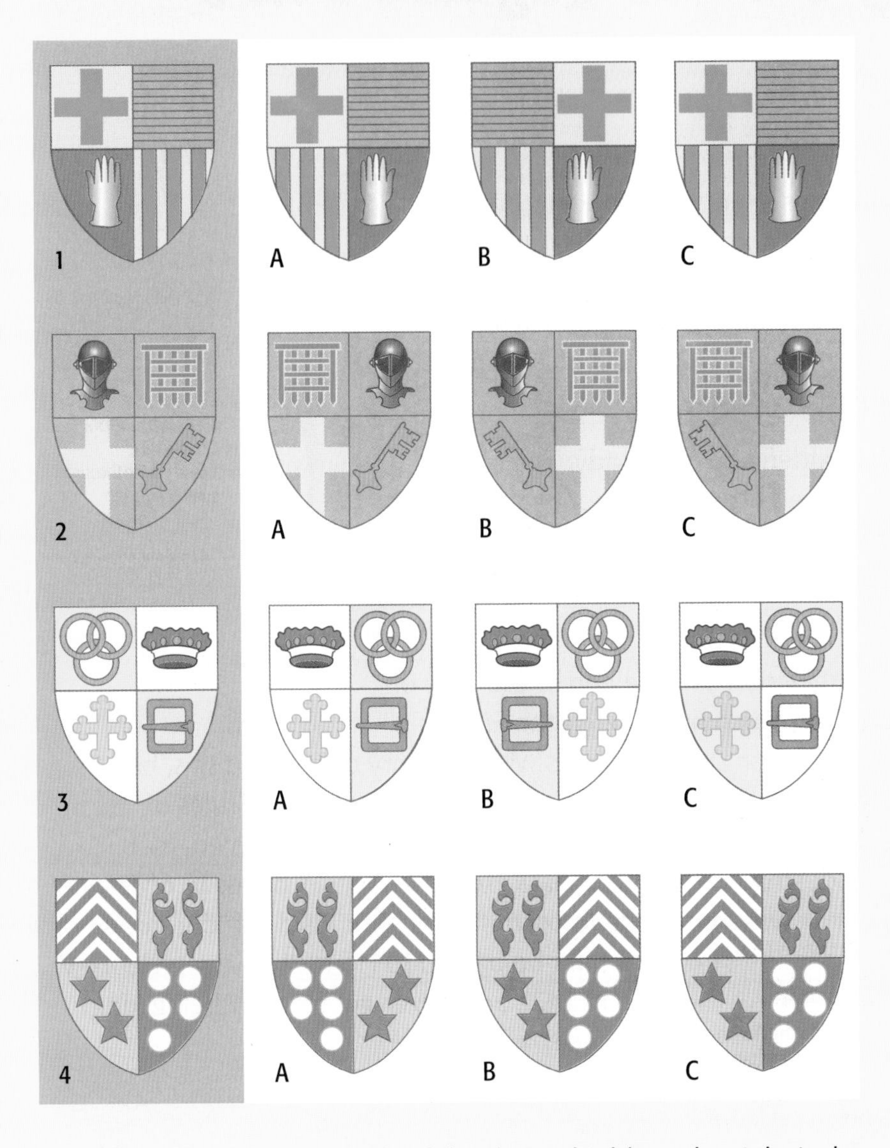

Look at these shields. Which of the three shields to the right is the correct mirror image? Tick your answers.

• TOP TIPS •

Use the Internet or the library to find out whether your family has its own coat of arms.

DID YOU KNOW?

The three lions on the England football and cricket shirts come from the badge of the royal family of England. The first proper heraldic coat of arms was that of Richard I (1189–99). He was known as 'The Lionheart'.

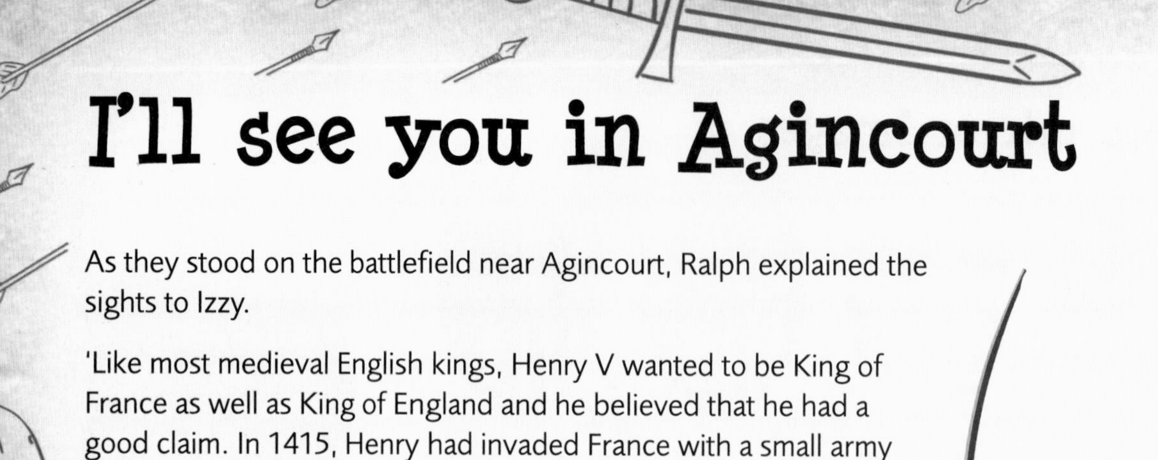

I'll see you in Agincourt

As they stood on the battlefield near Agincourt, Ralph explained the sights to Izzy.

'Like most medieval English kings, Henry V wanted to be King of France as well as King of England and he believed that he had a good claim. In 1415, Henry had invaded France with a small army and had taken the city of Harfleur, but he was met by a much larger French army and tried to retreat. On the 25th October he was forced to ready his troops near Agincourt.'

Longbow

Made of yew
Flexible and strong
Quick to fire
Could punch through suits of armour

'It had been raining and the battlefield was muddy. The heavily armoured French knights attacked. The French kept attacking but the English longbows were killing many of them. The French fought without much of a clear plan and, bogged down in the mud, they eventually lost about 6000 knights.'

'In many ways, the Battle of Agincourt saw the end of the "age of chivalry". During the battle, the French had robbed the English "baggage train" and killed the English drummer boys. When Henry discovered this, he ordered that the French prisoners be killed. All of these acts were against the rules of chivalry. Most importantly, however, the English longbows, fired by ordinary men, had destroyed the upper class French knights. Charles VI of France was then made to promise that after his death the throne of France would be passed to Henry. However, Henry V died in 1422 and never got to enjoy being king of France.'

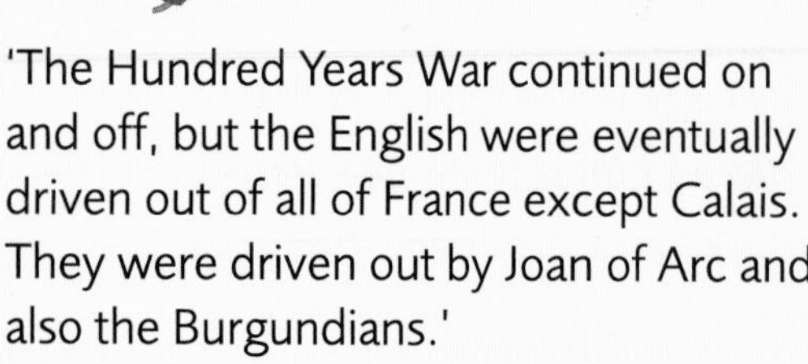

Crossbow

Used by the French
Accurate and powerful
Slow to load

'The Hundred Years War continued on and off, but the English were eventually driven out of all of France except Calais. They were driven out by Joan of Arc and also the Burgundians.'

'Wow,' said Izzy. 'Finally, a *woman* to learn about. I am going to find out more.'

Agincourt line-up

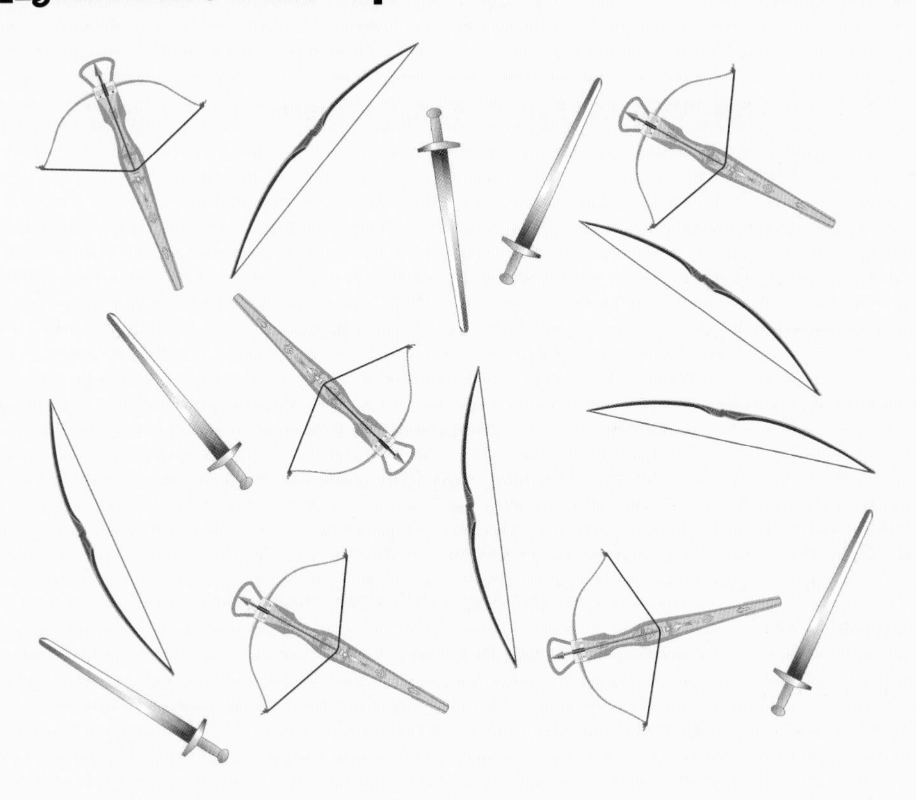

Draw ***only*** three straight lines on the drawing above to divide it into five sections. Each section must have one longbow, one crossbow and one sword.

• TOP TIPS •

Try to identify the key reason for the French loss at Agincourt. Was it:

- **the weather?**
- **the longbow?**
- **good English leadership?**
- **bad French leadership?**

Impossible, isn't it? This is because, in history, things often happen due to a combination of reasons.

DID YOU KNOW?

Many of Henry V's soldiers were suffering so badly from diarrhoea that they had to cut the bottoms out of their trousers for ease of access!

Test your knowledge 6

1 Fill in the gaps.

a) .... was the English King who 'started' the Hundred Years War.

b) Edward's first main battle was ....

c) Edward's second main battle was ....

d) Henry V was the English King who fought the Battle of ....

e) Henry V made the French King .... promise him the throne of France.

f) .... and the Burgundians defeated the English.

g) Stories about .... were very popular with knights.

h) King Arthur supposedly had a .... table.

i) The playwright .... wrote a famous play about Henry V.

j) Edward III was very keen on the knightly rules of chivalry and he invented the ....

(10 marks)

2 Fill in the missing dates of numbers.

a) The Hundred Years War was not 100 years long. It was fought between about .... to ....

b) The Battle of Crecy was fought in ....

c) The Battle of Poitiers was fought in ....

d) The Battle of Agincourt was fought in ....

e) Henry V died in ....

f) The battles of the Hundred Years War are different from the Battle of Hastings because they took place nearly .... years later.

g) Only .... people can be in the Order of the Garter at any one time.

h) Richard I was the first English King to have a proper 'heraldic coat of arms'. He ruled from ....

(8 marks)

3 Answer these questions with one word or a short sentence.

a) What is the name for the two animals which hold up the shield on a coat of arms?

....

b) What are the words called at the bottom of a coat of arms?

....

c) What four items would a knight display his arms on?

....

d) What is the study and design of coats of arms called?

....

e) What design famously features on England football shirts because of Richard I?

....

(5 marks)

4 Circle the odd one out. Then give a reason why it is the odd one out.

a) A Crest   B Motto   C Mantelpiece   D Shield

....

b) A Edward III   B Henry V   C Richard I   D Charles VI

....

c) A Hastings   B Agincourt   C Crecy   D Poitiers

....

d) A Longbow   B Machine gun   C Crossbow   D Sword

....

e) A Baxinet   B Knee flap   C Gauntlets   D Solleret

....

(5 marks)

(Total 28 marks)

Girl power

'It's my turn to teach you a few things,' said Izzy. She had asked Ralph, Max and Spotless to sit around the kitchen table and had set up a flip chart which she was pointing at with a long stick.

'Look, you sexist men, there were loads of important women in the Middle Ages. Your books don't seem to mention any women at all except as mothers and wives. Well, look at these.

1 Queen Matilda, England (ruled 1102–1116). This woman was rock hard. She was named as Queen of England, but her miserable cousin Stephen tried to take the throne from her. She fought him for years and her son became the next King of England.

2 Hildegard of Bingen, Germany (1098–1179). She wrote books, founded nunneries and wrote music. She had thousands of followers.

3 Joan of Arc, France (1412–1431). She was just a peasant girl, but she dressed in armour, led the French army and beat the English over and over in the Hundred Years War. She was caught and burned as a witch by the English.

4 Julian of Norwich, England (1342–1416). She was an English hermit and mystic. She had religious visions and never left her tiny room, ever. She was made a saint and wrote a book which many religious people read.

5 Eleanor of Aquitaine, France (1122–1204). She was King Richard Lionheart's mother. She had two husbands, fought her own wars and went on Crusade. She was one of the most powerful people in Europe for much of the 1100s.

6 Trotula of Salerno, Italy (11th century). She was a professor of medicine in Italy and wrote many books to help male doctors treat sick women.

7 Melisende, France (1105–1160). She ran the French kingdom in Jerusalem. She fought both her husband and then her son for the right to do so and won. Even when her son finally got control of Jerusalem, she made herself his advisor.'

Medieval women mix-up!

Solve the anagrams and then match up the left column with the right column.

1 TUTTRLAO	Ran Jerusalem
2 IFNLIANJUORWOCH	Was a medical writer
3 DIMNELSEE	Queen of England
4 OEELNRA	Fought and defeated the English
5 TLAMAID	Wrote music and books
6 ARJNOFCOA	Stayed in one room all of her life
7 EGAEHILRDD	Lionheart's mum (very powerful)

• TOP TIPS •

Do some of your own research into one of the women mentioned here. Research is one of the most important skills that you need in order to be an historian.

DID YOU KNOW?

Some people claim that there was even a Pope who was a woman. The first known reference to Pope John/Joan occurs in the thirteenth century, 350 years after her supposed reign. According to legend, she pretended to be a man for her whole life and was only discovered when she gave birth during a parade.

Robin who?

Ralph had settled down to watch his favourite film. It was about Robin Hood and most of the characters were played by Americans with iffy English accents. Izzy walked in and said, 'None of this is true,' and wandered out again. Ralph finished the film and went to see Max for reassurance.

'Sorry, sir, but Robin Hood is an example of a folk myth or a legend. However, these types of stories can tell us a lot about the period they come from. The Robin Hood story tells us that King John was unpopular. It also tells us that the laws that applied to royal forests were hated by the people. People wanted a Robin Hood, so they invented one.

The story
Robin, a nobleman's son, returns from the Crusades to find King John's evil Sheriff of Nottingham ruling the land harshly. Robin and his merry men hide in Sherwood Forest (Little John, Friar Tuck, Will Scarlett and Maid Marian). They defeat the evil Sheriff, rob from the rich and give to the poor.

The reality
Robin Hood is probably a mixture of all sorts of stories about outlaws in the Middle Ages. Some of these stories make him a nobleman and some a yeoman. These various stories have Robin living in many different places. There were various people who could have been called Sheriff of Nottingham but none of them quite fit in with the story.

Sporting history

The main purpose of forests like Sherwood was as a venue for noblemen to hunt in. In fact, most medieval sports had some element of violence, danger or bloodshed in them. Try to match the definitions on the left with the medieval sporting terms on the right.

1. The medieval sport of attacking your opponent's shins with your feet.
2. A sport for the upper classes whereby a bird of prey is released from the wrist to kill animals.
3. Hunting these huge wild pigs was a favourite pastime for noble hunters. These enormous, fast pigs were armed with huge, dangerous tusks and could be very heavy.
4. A sport where a pack of large, savage dogs were set upon an even larger animal and bets were placed on the resulting fights.
5. Two male chickens were placed in an enclosed space and would fight to the death using the large 'claws' on their 'ankles'. Bets were placed.
6. A huge dog bred for chasing and pulling down deer.
7. A game much like modern rounders. Not normally dangerous!
8. A game which could take place over a huge area with very few rules. One village played another and violence was a frequent occurrence.

- Bear baiting or Bull baiting
- Cock fighting
- Shin hacking
- Deer hound
- Trapball
- Falconry
- Football
- Boar hunting

DID YOU KNOW?

Many modern expressions come from the sport of falconry.

- **'Fed up' refers to a falcon that has been given enough food so that it won't bother to hunt.**
- **A 'cadger' was an old falconer who could not manage the more difficult jobs (hence 'old codger').**
- **The phrase 'to hoodwink someone' (or fool someone) is named after the action of hooding a bird's eyes to take its prey away from it.**

• TOP TIPS •

Why not go to a falconry display? There are many falconry centres that put on displays for the public, and they may even let you fly the birds yourself.

King John

'Robin Hood might not be real, but King John was a real king.' Izzy was really getting in to this medieval stuff.

Some people say that he was a really useless King of England. He reigned from 1199 to 1216. He was called Lackland from the age of about two, when in 1169, his father, Henry II, divided up his dominions between his three older sons – Henry the Younger, Richard and Geoffrey. He was also called Softsword because he lost lots of battles.

'One time, and this is my favourite, he lost all of his treasure in the mud while crossing an estuary. People still search for it today.'

'Also, did you know his brother was Richard the Lionheart and his Mother was the great Eleanor of Aquitaine?'

'One good thing did happen during John's reign. The barons forced him to sign the Magna Carta in 1215. The name Magna Carta is Latin – it means "Great Charter". It took some power away from the king and gave many rights and freedoms to the people.'

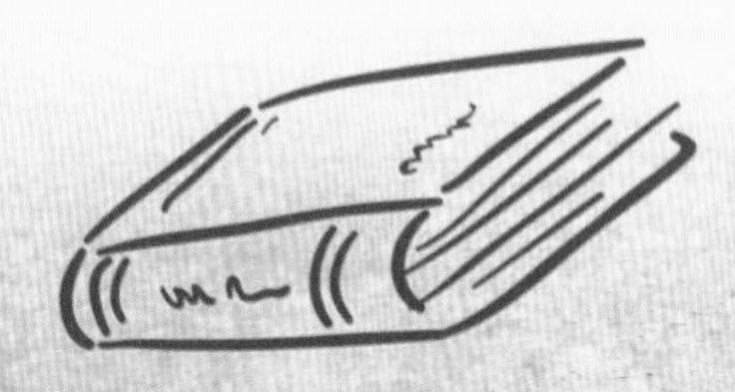

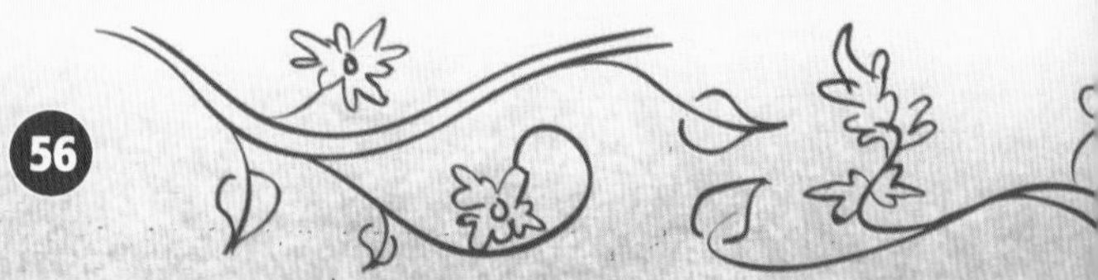

John's text message

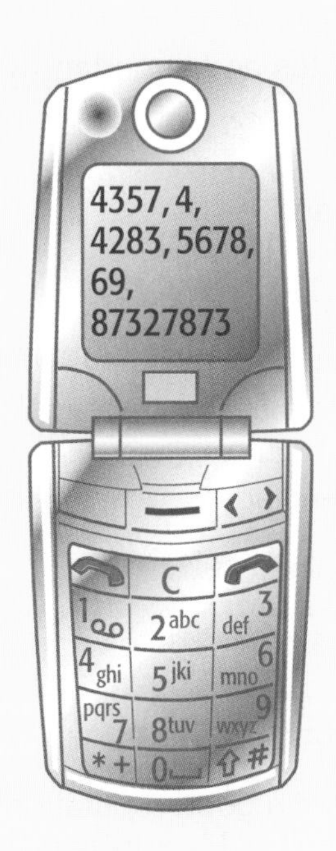

Use the phone pad below to work out King John's text message.

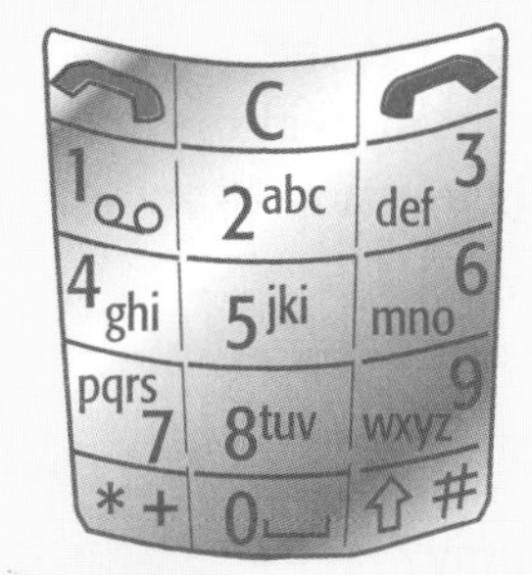

• TOP TIPS •

The term 'The Crusades' refers to a very lengthy series of wars between the Christian West and the Muslim 'Middle East'. The first Crusade was called for by Pope Urban II in 1095 when he asked for soldiers to volunteer to recapture Jerusalem. By 1270, there had been eight crusades and a children's crusade. Sometimes Crusaders never made it anywhere near Jerusalem and instead sacked and looted Jewish or other Christian cities. The thousands of children's crusaders set off in boats from Marseilles and were never heard of again!

DID YOU KNOW?

John's brother, King Richard I, was King of England for 10 years. During that time he only visited England twice, for less than a year. He spent most of his time in France or on Crusade.

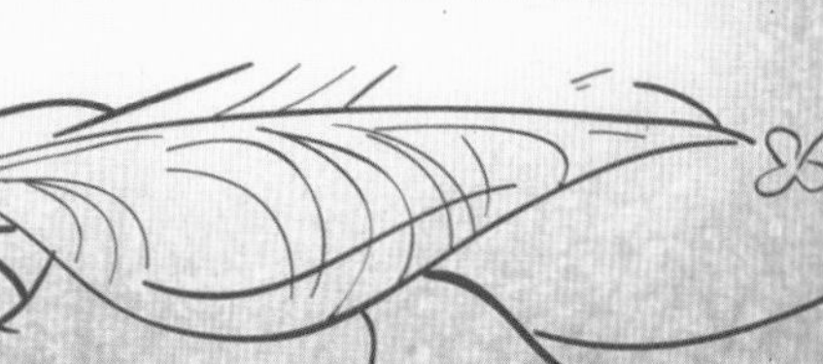

Test your knowledge 7

1 Fill in the missing dates and important women.

a) Melisende was .... when she died.

b) .... and .... were alive in the 11th Century.

c) Hildegard of Bingham died in ....

d) .... was born in 1412.

e) .... arguably ruled England from 1102 to 1116.

f) Julian of Norwich died in ....

g) Eleanor of Aquitaine was .... when she died.

(7 marks)

2 Fill in the missing words.

King John has not got a good reputation. Two of his nicknames are .... and .... This is because he lost battles and much of England's lands in France. Magna Carta is .... and means .... It was signed by King John in .... It was the .... who made him sign. The Magna Carta was an important step in the development of English politics. King John is also known for losing his treasure in an ....

(7 marks)

3 Answer these questions with one word or a short sentence.

a) In the Robin Hood stories who is Robin's arch enemy?

....

b) Robin Hood was probably not real but is an example of what kind of story?

....

c) Robin Hood is probably a mixture of stories about what kind of person in the Middle Ages?

....

d) What laws were so unpopular that they may have led to Robin Hood stories becoming popular?

....

e) Who was the unpopular king who was the Sheriff of Nottingham's boss?

....

(5 marks)

4 True or false?

a) Women were not important in the Middle Ages. ....

b) Joan of Arc was a young peasant girl who led an army. ....

c) You can still buy CDs of Hildegard of Bingen's music. ....

d) A mystic is a religious person who has visions. ....

e) A hermit has lots of friends. ....

f) Robin Hood stories always show Robin dressed in orange. ....

g) Little Pete is one of Robin's gang. ....

h) King John was known as Shortsword. ....

i) King John lost his treasure down the toilet. ....

(9 marks)

(Total 28 marks)

Gael warning

Izzy had gone to visit her Aunt Siân in Wales. Siân was able to teach her some medieval Welsh history.

'The people of Wales are descended from the Celts, who were the original inhabitants of England. When the Romans and then the Saxons invaded, they drove the native English population into Wales and Cornwall. After that, the relationship between the people of Wales and the people of England was very strained. The King of Mercia, a man called Offa, built a long ditch to keep the Welsh out of England in Saxon times. It was called Offa's Dyke. Here's a timeline for the Middle Ages. All these events occurred after the Saxon invasion.'

Siân passed over a book for Izzy to look at.

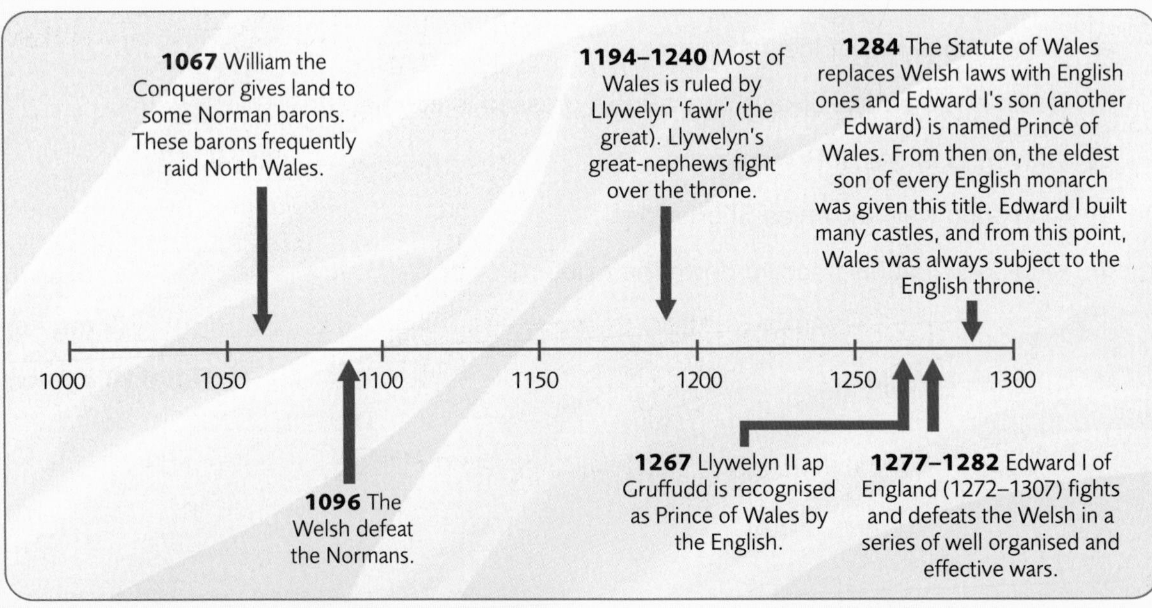

Caerphilly castle

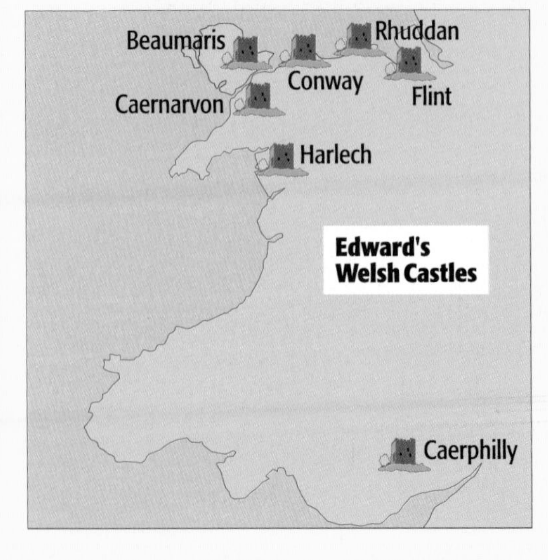

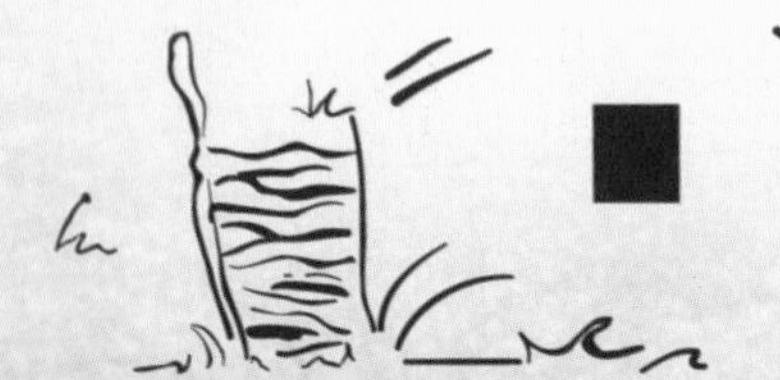

Beaumaris Castle

James of St George, Edward I's chief architect, has lost his bucket and trowel. Can you solve the Beaumaris Castle maze to help him find it?

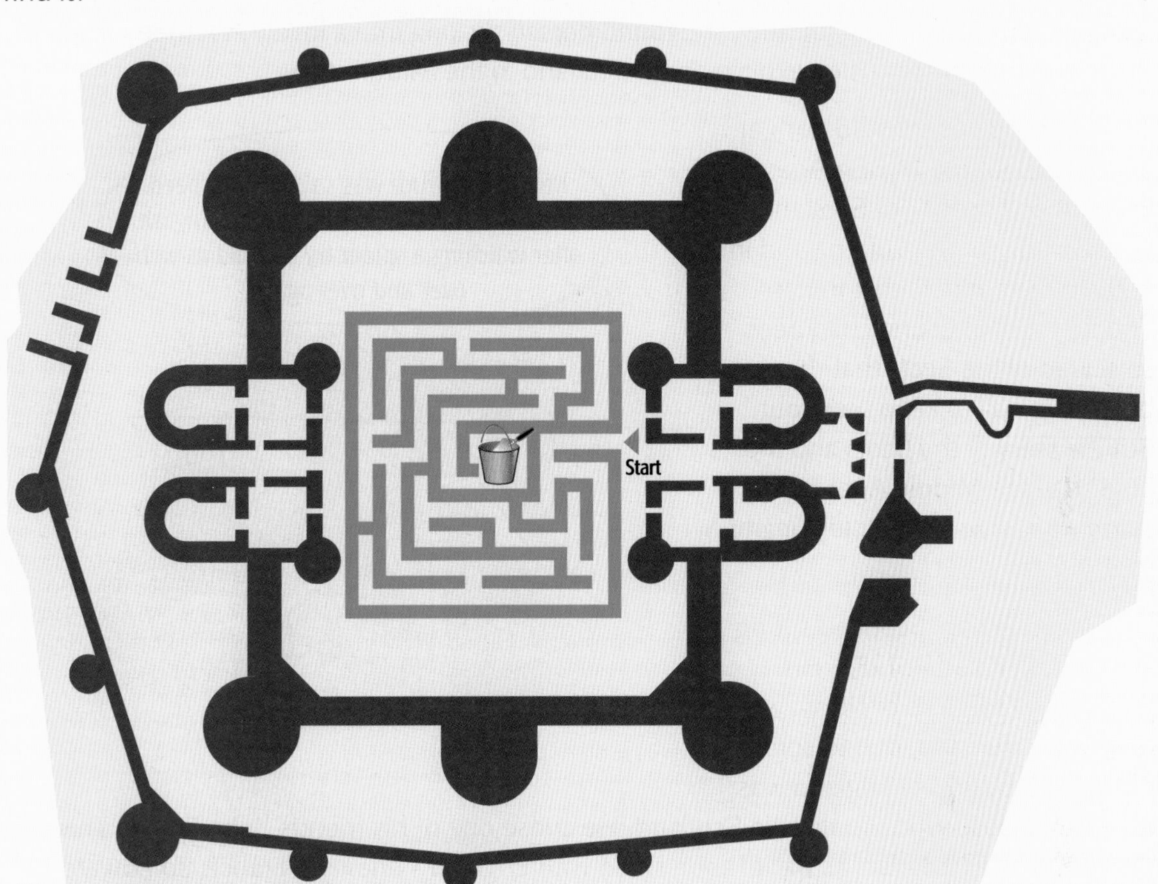

• TOP TIPS •

At this point in English history, there are three Edwards one after the other. Try to think of a way to tell them apart. Perhaps make up your own nicknames. For example:

- **Strong Edward – Edward I (1272–1307)**
- **Weak Edward – Edward II (1307–1327)**
- **Strong, chivalric Edward – Edward III (1327–1377)**

DID YOU KNOW?

Edward I, like King John I, had a number of nicknames. He was known as Longshanks because of his height and as The Hammer of the Scots because of his victories in Scotland.

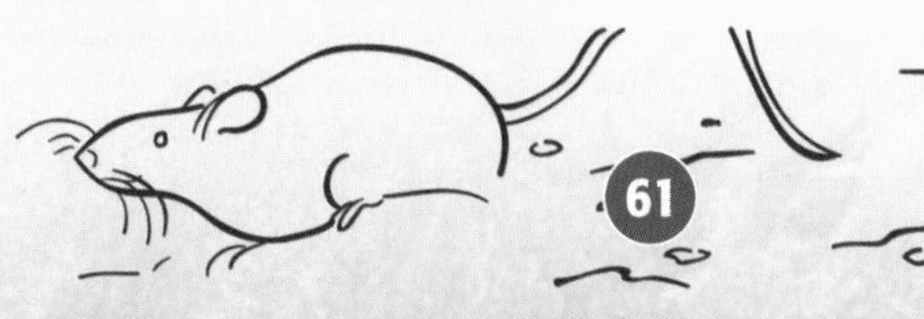
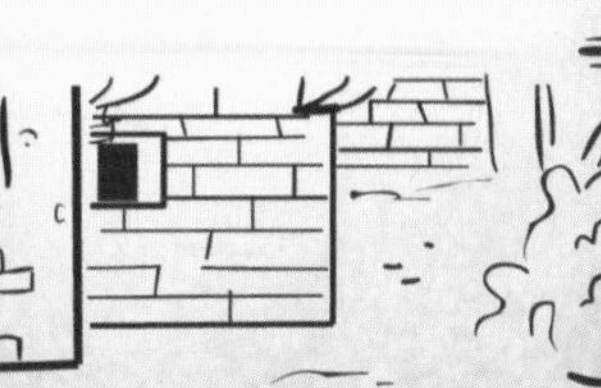

Bannockburnt!

Izzy knew that cousin Lesley would be very jealous if she didn't go and find out about Scotland too. After a long journey, she found herself tucking into a lovely Aberdeen Angus steak and listening to Lesley explain about Scotland in the Middle Ages.

'Scotland and England did not get on throughout the Middle Ages. Even when James VI of Scotland became King James I of England in 1603, it did not help that much. The Romans, of course, had been so scared of the Scots that they built a big wall to keep them out. But the story of the Scots and the English in the Middle Ages really starts with Edward I.' Lesley nearly spat the name out.

Lesley continued, 'Scotland's King Alexander III died in 1286. His successor, Margaret of Norway, died soon after and, due to some old laws, Edward I of England was asked to choose who should rule Scotland. He chose one of his friends, John Balliol. This proved to be a bad plan, as Balliol soon sided with England's enemy – France, so Edward I marched north and defeated Balliol. Edward stole the Stone of Scone and the Scottish Crown Jewels. He appointed a governor to rule.'

Lesley continued, 'But William Wallace, a Scottish leader, fought back. You may have seen a film about this bit. Edward caught Wallace and had him chopped into bits and his body sent around Scotland.

When Edward I died, his weak son Edward II lost to the great leader Robert the Bruce at the battle of Bannockburn. Bruce became King of Scotland and Scotland remained independent of England for 400 more years.'

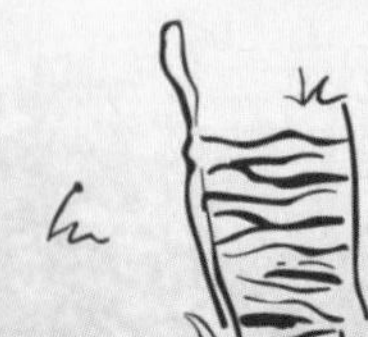
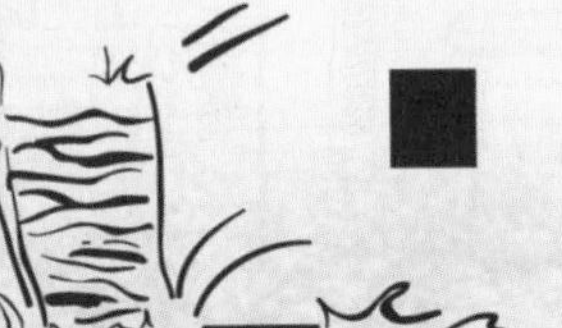

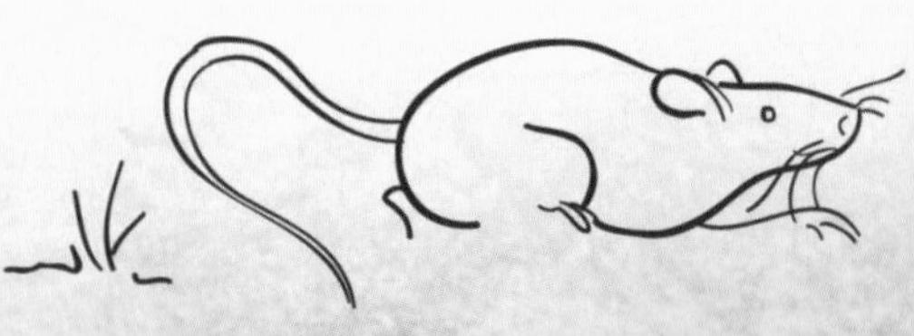

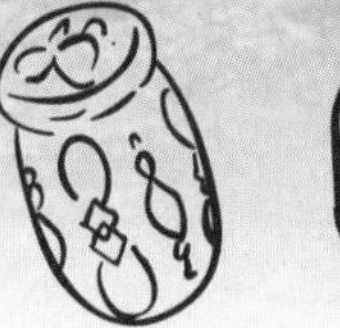

Scottish crossword

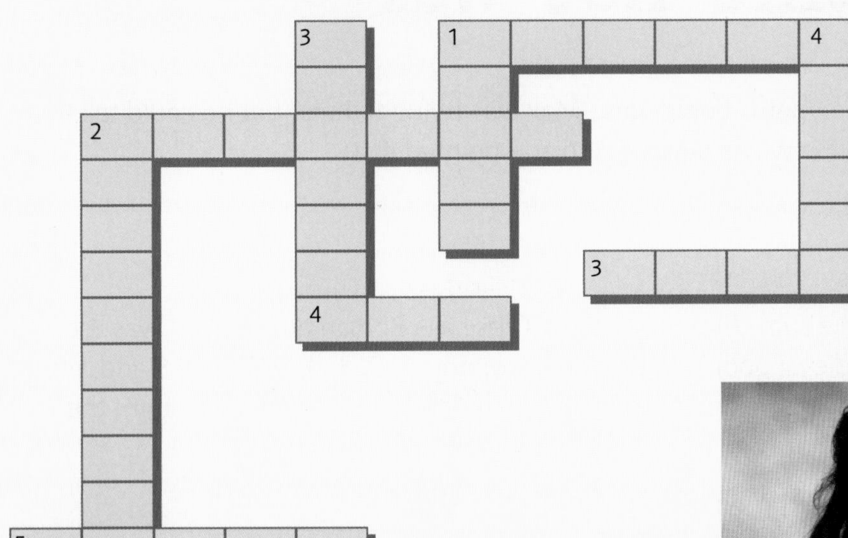

Mel Gibson as William Wallace in *Braveheart*

Across

1 Robert the Bruce watched a _ _ _ _ _ _ .

2 John _ _ _ _ _ _ _ ruled Scotland for Edward I.

3 Someone from Scotland can be called a _ _ _ _ .

4 _ _ _ Gibson played Wallace in the film *Braveheart*.

5 Edward I stole the _ _ _ _ _ Jewels from Scotland.

Down

1 The Stone of _ _ _ _ _ is a symbol of the Scottish Kings.

2 Edward II lost the Battle of _ _ _ _ _ _ _ _ _ _ _ _ .

3 _ _ _ _ _ _ _ Wallace was a Scottish leader.

4 _ _ _ _ _ _ the Bruce was another Scottish leader.

• TOP TIPS •

If you watch a film about real historical events, always check the facts afterwards. Most so-called historical films mess around with the facts to create a better story.

DID YOU KNOW?

The blockbuster film *Braveheart* is based on the life of William Wallace. It features the actor Mel Gibson as Wallace.

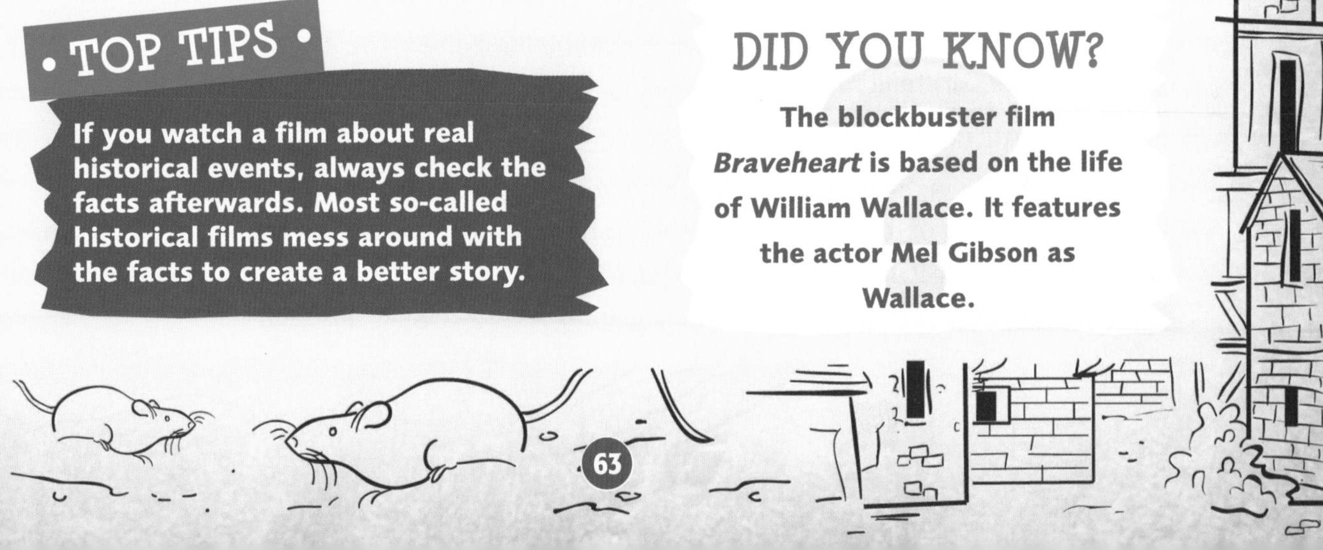

Make sums not war

Izzy was struggling with her maths homework. Max was trying to help, but he could tell that Izzy was about to give up. He wrote down a sum and pointed at it:

MMMCCCXXX – MMXXIX

'Do that one,' he said.

Izzy could clearly not do the sum. Max explained, 'These are Roman numerals. It was the Arabs who taught the medieval people to do sums properly. 1, 2, 3, 4, 5, 6, 7, 8, 9 and, most importantly, 0 are Arabic numbers and make maths so much easier. Arabs also taught the Westerners algebra...'

'So that's who to blame,' interrupted Izzy.

'...and astronomy,' continued Max. 'In fact, when the Crusaders were not fighting the Muslim Arabs they gained an awful lot from them. Here is a list of things.'

Max wrote down this list and Izzy doodled some pictures.
'It makes you wonder what they were fighting about if they had so much to teach each other,' pointed out Izzy.

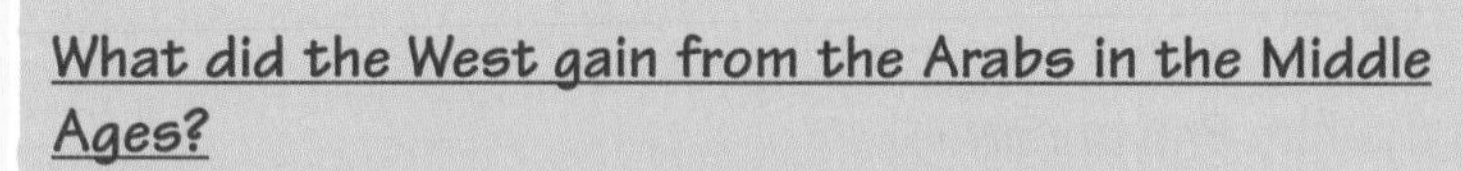
What did the West gain from the Arabs in the Middle Ages?

Maths – algebra, numbers and the zero

Science – astronomy, navigation, compasses, chemistry

Architecture – improved castle building

Food – many spices, pepper, dates and various fruits, rice, coffee

Helpful household goods – pain-killing drugs, carpets, mirrors, wheelbarrows, paper, water clocks

Games – chess

Learning – many books by Greeks and Romans had been lost to the West, but there were many of these books to be found in Eastern libraries

Max said, 'People in the Middle Ages also borrowed ideas from China. Gunpowder and silk are good examples of this. But Westerners did have some important inventions of their own. They discovered gears, the crank, the water wheel, ways to make metals, rudders for ships and – the invention which perhaps helped end the Middle Ages – printing.'

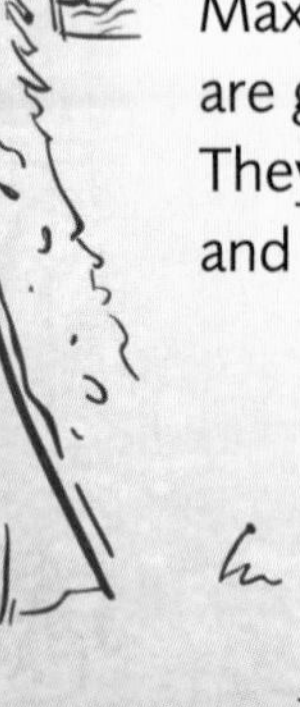
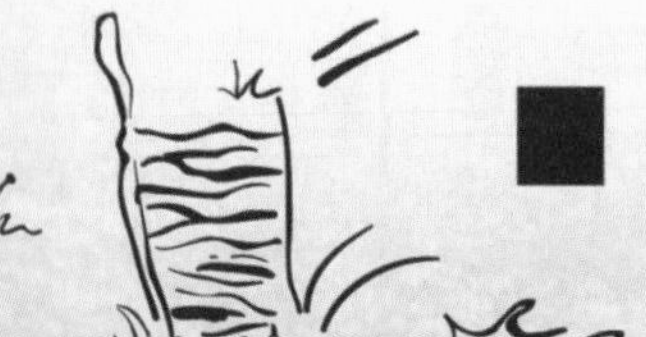
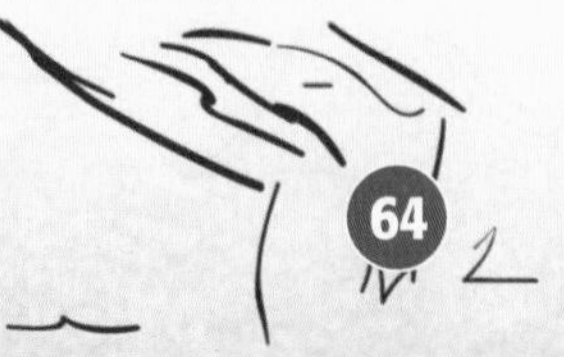
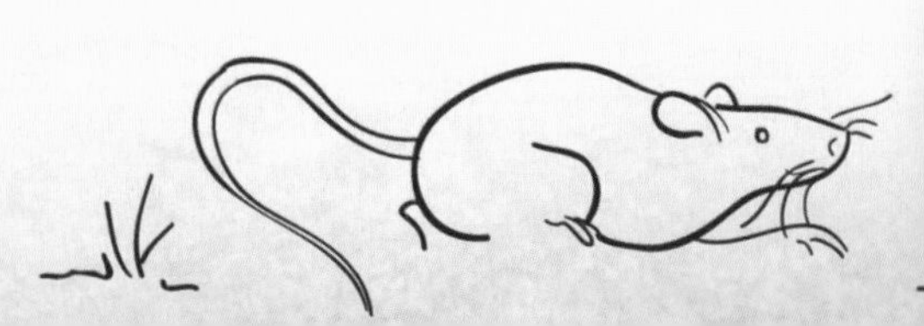

Roman-Arabic mathematical problems

1 = I	2 = II	3 = III	4 = IV	5 = V	6 = VI	7 = VII
8 = VIII	9 = IX	10 = X	50 = L	100 = C	500 = D	1000 = M

Change the Roman numerals below into Arabic numbers.

1 XXIV ....

2 XXX ....

3 MMVI ....

4 MLXVI ....

5 MCC ....

6 LXXIII ....

7 CCLXXII ....

8 CCCIII ....

9 MMMMMCCCCXXXIX ....

10 LXV ....

• TOP TIPS •

- **Before the invention of the printing press, information could not be distributed in the way it is today. Peasants in the Middle Ages would have got their knowledge of events from:**

  – Rumour
  – Gossip
  – Stories
  – Later, through sermons at church.

- **Try to imagine life without easy access to written information like books or newspapers. This could help you to imagine what it would be like to live in the Middle Ages.**

DID YOU KNOW?

Two important inventions can be used to mark the beginning and the end of the Middle Ages:

1 In the beginning of the period the stirrup was introduced for horses, making fighting on horseback easier and therefore introducing the knight.

2 The printing press helped to spread information and learning and, as such, brought about the end of the Middle Ages.

Test your knowledge 8

1 Cross out the incorrect words.

a) *Edward I/Edward II* built many castles in Wales.

b) His chief castle architect was *George of St James/James of St George*.

c) Edward was known as *Shorty/Longshanks* and also *The Hammer of the Scots/The Hammer of the Welsh*.

d) The eldest son of the English monarch is known as *The Duke of Wales/The Prince of Wales*.

e) Offa, King of Mercia, built a big earthwork which is named after him. It is called *Offa's Pike/Offa's Dyke*.

f) Between 1194 and 1240 Llywelyn Fawr ruled Wales. Fawr means *fierce/great*.

g) Edward I was a *strong/weak* king. Edward II was a *strong/weak* king. Edward III was a *strong/weak* king.

h) The *Scone of Stone/Stone of Scone* is the symbol of Scottish kingship.

i) *Wadham/Balliol* was asked to rule Scotland on the death of the last Scottish monarch.

j) *Bannockburn/Hastings* was the decisive battle for Scotland in the period.

(10 marks)

2 Fill in the missing date.

a) Edward I died in ....

b) Edward II died in ....

c) The Welsh defeated the Normans in ....

d) Llywelyn II ap Gruffudd was recognised as Prince of Wales in ....

e) In .... the Statute of Wales replaced Welsh laws with English ones.

f) King Alexander III of Scotland died in ....

g) James I of Scotland became James VI of England in ....

h) Edward III died in ....

i) William the Conqueror awarded land to some barons in ....

j) Scotland remained independent from England after Bannockburn for .... years.

(10 marks)

3 Answer these questions with one word or a short sentence.

a) What type of numbers were in use in the Middle Ages before the Crusades?

....

b) The Crusades were fought between which two major world religions?

....

c) Which English King wore three lions as his symbol?

....

d) Name the game of logic, skill and tactics that the Arabs probably taught the Crusaders.

....

e) What branch of mathematics did the Crusaders learn from the Arabs?

....

(5 marks)

4 Circle the odd one out. Then give a reason why it is the odd one out.

	A	B	C	D
a)	A M	B P	C I	D V
b)	A Pain-killers	B Spices	C Dates	D Edam
c)	A William Wallace	B Robert the Bruce	C Margaret of Norway	D Mel Gibson
d)	A Gears	B Cranks	C Playstation	D Compass
e)	A Millennium Stadium	B Flint	C Harlech	D Conway

(5 marks)

(Total 30 marks)

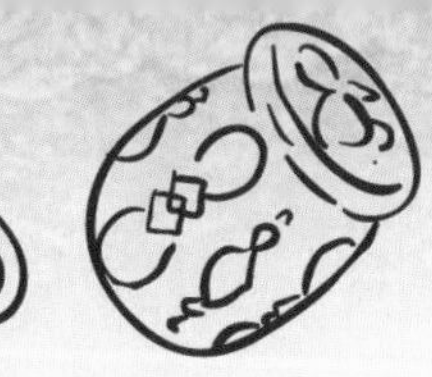

Vomiting, dizziness and buboes

'I remember something interesting about the Middle Ages,' said Ralph after breakfast. 'The Black Death!'

'Sounds horrible,' said Izzy.

'The Black Death arrived in Europe in 1347 and England in 1348,' explained Ralph. 'In some parts of England, it killed as many as one in three people. Most of Britain, except Northern Scotland, was affected and millions of people throughout Europe died.'

'How did it kill so many people?' Izzy was interested now.

'It was a disease that gave you little chance of survival. There were a number of symptoms: fever, headaches, vomiting, dizziness and worst of all buboes.'

'Yuck. They even *sound* grim, what were they?'

'Black lumps, sometimes the size of tennis balls that developed in your armpits and your groin. The people were terrified. They hadn't got the scientific knowledge or skills to find the cause or to cure the disease. Some said that God was angry, some blamed foreigners, some blamed the planets. They tried potions, chants and all sorts of magic charms to cure or prevent the plague, but it struck rich and poor alike. One group called flagellants even tried whipping themselves over and over again. The dead were simply chucked into huge burial pits.'

Ralph continued, 'Historians and doctors today think that the Black Death was a disease called Bubonic Plague. This disease is spread by the fleas that live on black rats. But there is some doubt about this explanation. After 1347 the plague never really went away. People built up a natural resistance to it, but there were outbreaks throughout the rest of the period and another particularly bad one happened in the 1660s. Antibiotics can cure it these days.'

Plague - true or false?

Draw a line to the healthy monk if the statement is true.

Draw a line to the grave if it is false.

1 The plague gave you buboes which were massive black boils.

2 The plague killed 1000 Scottish people.

3 The plague was also known as the Blue Death.

7 The plague killed one in three people in some parts of England.

4 People blamed the planets.

5 The plague was carried by fleas.

6 Plague fleas lived on cats.

• TOP TIPS •

We can learn a lot about different societies from the way they dealt with disease. For example, the Romans built aqueducts, bathhouses and sewers showing that they were practical and well organised. Whereas, the people of the Middle Ages prayed, whipped themselves and persecuted foreigners. This is a simplified argument but revealing nonetheless.

DID YOU KNOW?

There are no longer any black rats *(Rattus rattus)* living in Britain. The rat that we all see in Britain is the brown rat *(Rattus norvegicus)*.

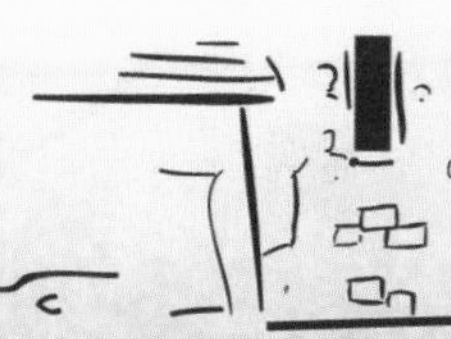
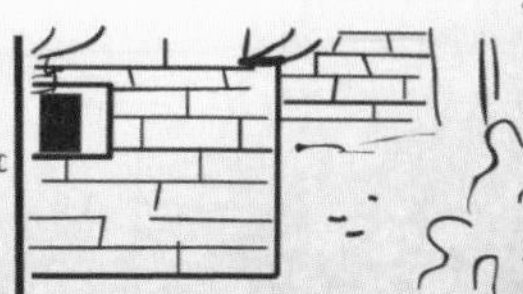

The peasants are revolting

Max joined in with the discussion.

'The Black Death changed everything. Firstly, the survivors thought that they had been specially chosen by God. Secondly, there had been so many deaths that there weren't enough people to work on the land any more. The peasants suddenly found that they were in a strong bargaining position and began to ask for better conditions and much higher wages from their lords. Those who didn't get what they wanted simply went elsewhere. King Edward III was so worried about the extra power of the peasants that, in 1351, he invented some laws called the Statute of Labourers. These tried to limit peasants' rising wages. But it was Edward's son, Richard II, who really had problems with the peasants. They had a revolt.'

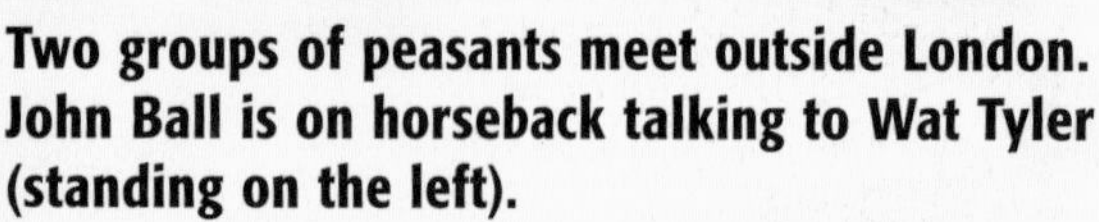

Two groups of peasants meet outside London. John Ball is on horseback talking to Wat Tyler (standing on the left).

The death of Wat Tyler. Richard II is shown twice – once riding towards the rebels, and once supervising the execution.

'In the summer of 1381, a peasant called Wat Tyler and a priest called John Ball led an army of peasants to London. The peasants didn't want to pay for the new taxes as the money was just being used to attack the French. They also hated the Statute of Labourers and marched to London to do something about it. They smashed palaces and killed noblemen on the way. When they got to London the king was in a difficult position and said that he would agree to their demands.'

'The peasants were revolting? Richard II didn't sound very nice, either!'

'The peasants still did not go home and Richard II rode out to meet them supported by some soldiers and nobles. No one is quite sure what happened next, but for some reason the Mayor of London killed Tyler. The peasant army strung their bows. Richard rode to them and made a speech which changed their minds. He promised them freedom and better conditions, and the peasants went home. However, Richard broke his promises and had the leaders horribly executed and hung up around London.'

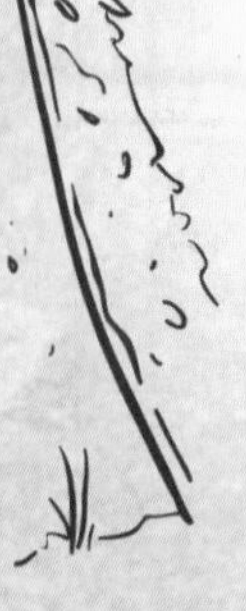   

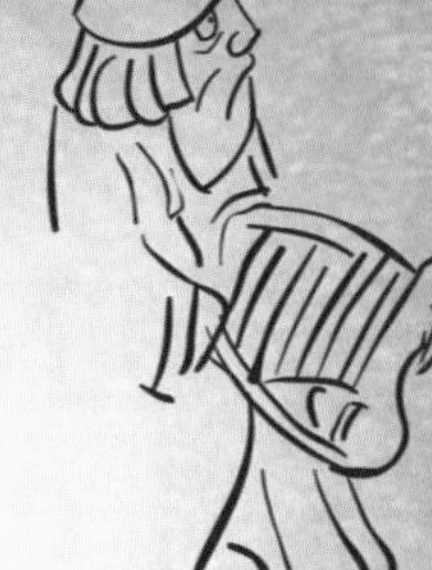

Peasants' Revolt wordsearch

J	B	U	I	P	E	A	S	A	N	T
P	O	L	M	B	C	E	Q	D	G	S
O	R	C	A	W	T	Y	L	E	R	T
A	I	P	Y	C	M	O	P	R	B	A
N	C	Y	R	H	K	V	B	E	E	T
L	H	B	G	A	C	D	A	T	E	U
T	A	X	E	S	S	E	E	R	N	T
U	R	O	N	V	R	E	V	A	F	E
L	D	N	F	O	T	Y	N	U	T	P
I	Y	B	Y	C	D	C	F	Q	V	H
H	J	A	O	I	U	N	T	R	E	N
C	M	W	K	H	J	U	O	C	Z	O
P	L	J	O	H	N	B	A	L	L	A

1 LONDON
2 TYLER
3 RICHARD
4 TAXES
5 BLACK DEATH
6 QUARTERED
7 JOHN BALL
8 STATUTE
9 PEASANT
10 MAYOR

• TOP TIPS •

The Peasants' Revolt is a good example of popular protest. This feature of English life becomes more and more important over the centuries.

DID YOU KNOW?

The most common method of execution used during this period was 'hanging, drawing and quartering':

First hang the victim until nearly dead.

Then slice the victim open and 'draw' out the stomach and intestines.

Then cut the victim into four.

Display the parts around town.

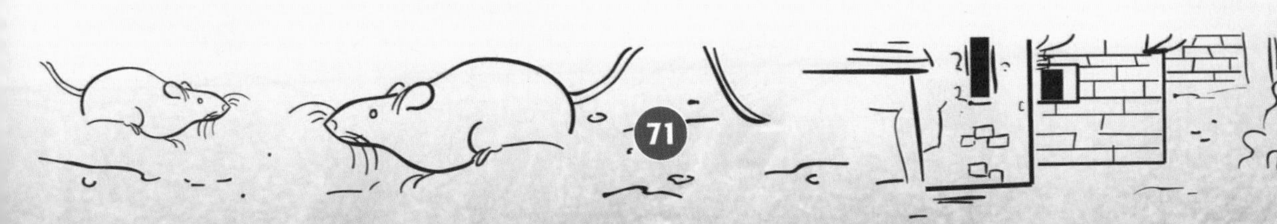

Nothing civil about your civil war!

'We must have looked at most of the important stuff from the Middle Ages in England,' said Izzy. 'I have to study the Tudors next at school. How do the Middle Ages end?'

As usual, Max knew all about it. 'The Middle Ages end in 1485 when Henry Tudor kills Richard III at the Battle of Bosworth and becomes Henry VII. The battle ends a series of devastating civil wars known as the Wars of the Roses.'

'Soft name for a series of horrible wars though,' pointed out Izzy.

Max explained, 'The York family had a white rose as their symbol and the Lancastrians had a red rose. Here are just a few of the key events.'

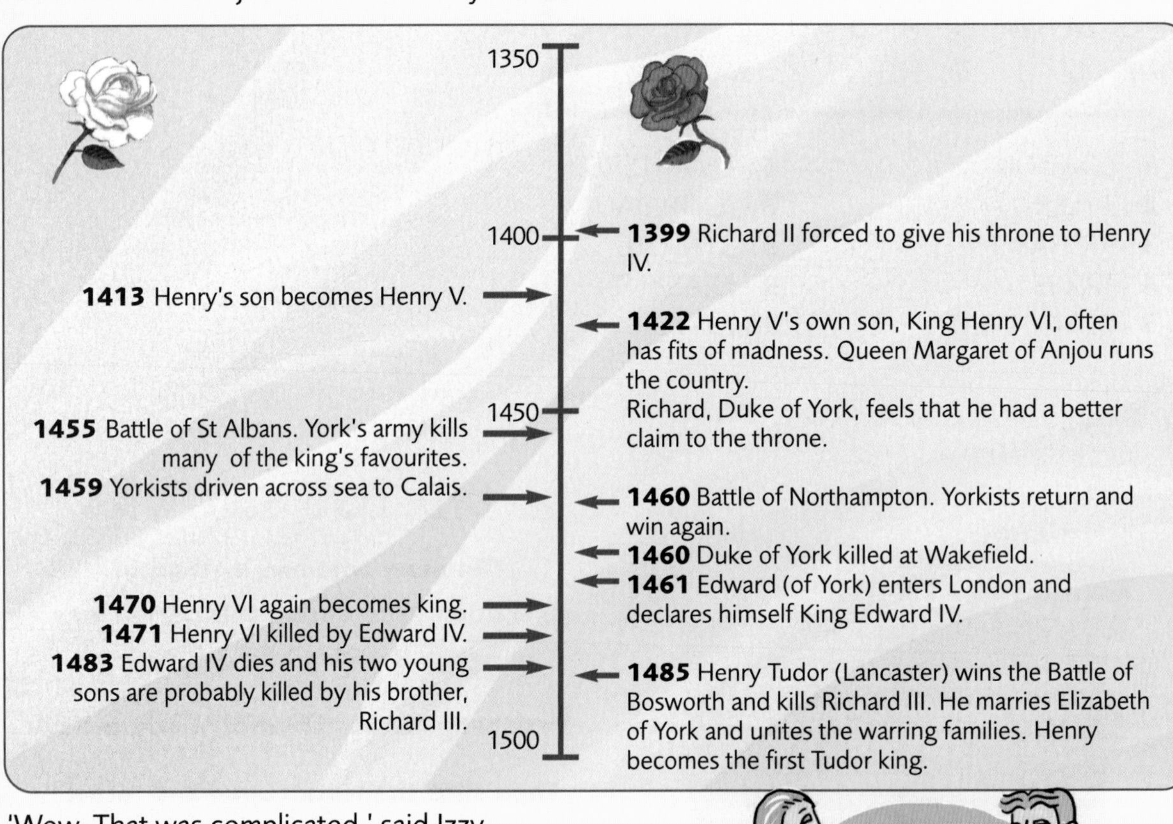

'Wow. That was complicated,' said Izzy.

'And that was only part of it,' answered Max. 'I hope that you have enjoyed your medieval studies, Izzy.'

'S'pose so.' Max figured that this was probably great praise from Izzy and went to make himself a cup of tea.

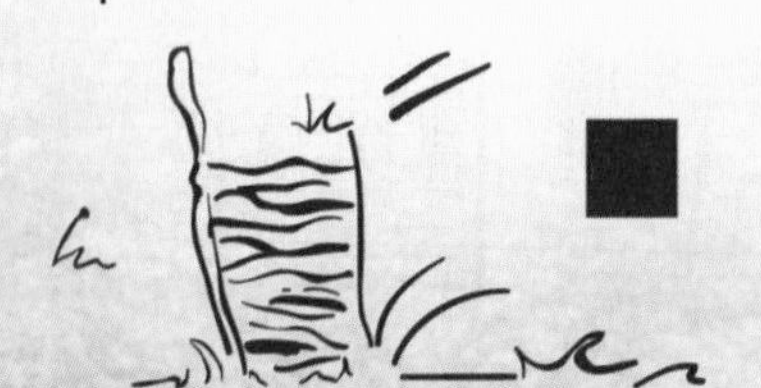

Rose gardening

Richard III and Henry VII are both holding their family symbol. But which roses are they holding?

DID YOU KNOW?

When Edward IV died in 1483, Richard III had Edward's sons (his heirs) placed in the Tower of London. This was the last time that they were seen alive. The skeletons of two boys were found in 1933. Many say that Richard had the boys killed so that he could be king (the story is that they were smothered with pillows). There is no proof, and a number of historians point out that he had no motive for doing so.

• TOP TIPS •

Remember that the Tudor Period is a name for a period in *English* history only. It is part of what historians call the Early Modern Period.

Revision special

Some medieval kings and queens of England have not been mentioned in this book. Here is a full list with a tiny bit of information about each one. Choose one or two to research.

Normans (named after Normandy in France)

William I (1066–1087). The Conqueror. A brave and ruthless leader who came from France and took the English throne. Died after falling from his horse.
William II (1087–1100). Ruddy of face. Died in a hunting 'accident'.
Henry I (1100–1135). Lost his son in a 'drink-sailing' accident.
Stephen (1135–1154). Fought for most of his reign with his cousin Matilda (Henry I's daughter).

Angevins (named after Anjou in France)

Henry II (1154–1189). Matilda's son. Did he order the death of Thomas Beckett? He started to organise the laws and workings of English government more effectively than his predecessors.
Richard I (1189–1199). The Lionheart. This Crusader king spent very little time in England. Died fighting in France.
John (1199–1216). Softsword, Lackland. Suffered the humiliation of the Magna Carta and lost all of his treasure and most of his battles. Died from overeating.

Plantagenets (family name)

Henry III (1216–1272). A weak and unimpressive man. He did much to try to civilise the English nation. He was much keener on the arts than on war.
Edward I (1272–1307). The Hammer of the Scots, Longshanks. A successful fighter and a hard king. Liked castles ... a lot.
Edward II (1307–1337). Weak and feeble. The court did not like the amount of power Edward gave to Piers Gaveston, a nobleman – so they had him killed. Lost to the Scots at Bannockburn. Murdered in a horrible way!
Edward III (1327–1377). Invented the chivalric Order of the Garter. A strong leader who won many battles.
Richard II (1377–1399) Became king at 10 years old. Faced down the Peasant's Revolt and was murdered by Henry IV.

The House of Lancaster (name and place)

Henry IV (1399–1413). Started badly by killing the previous king and had a troubled reign. Managed to pass the throne on to his son (which is quite good going considering he had no rightful claim to be king himself).
Henry V (1413–1422). Won many battles. Spent a lot of time fighting in France. Had a wild youth but was a serious king. Died young from dysentry.

Henry VI (1422–1471). Not a 'kingly' king. Lost most of France. Founded Eton and King's College Cambridge. Was murdered as part of the Wars of the Roses.

The House Of York (name and place)

Edward IV (1461–1483). Was heavily involved in a lot of the battles of the Wars of the Roses. Died of a fever.

Richard III (1483–1485). Shakespeare portrayed this man as an evil hunchback. Accused of killing his nephews to gain the throne. Died in battle at Bosworth after single-handedly charging Henry Tudor's army.

Test your knowledge 9

1 How many medieval kings were there? ....

2 Who reigned for the longest period? ....

3 Who reigned for the shortest period? ....

4 How many medieval Edwards were there? ....

5 How many medieval Williams were there? ....

6 Which dynasty (family) had the most kings? ....

7 Which dynasty the fewest? ....

8 Which kings were murdered? ....

9 What did John die of? ....

10 Which is your favourite king? ....

(Total 10 marks)

Glossary

Anachronism
When something is placed into the wrong time period, for example a digital watch on a Norman soldier.

Archer
A soldier who uses a bow and arrow.

Baron
A very important nobleman, below the king in the feudal system.

Biased
Describes information that is one-sided.

Black Death
The plague which hit medieval Europe.

Britannia
The Roman name for Great Britain.

Buboes
Boils in the armpit or groin caused by the Black Death.

Cause and consequence
A phrase used to point out the relationship between what makes an event happen and the results of that event.

Cavalry
Soldiers who fight from horseback.

Charter
A medieval law document.

Chivalry
The rules that a knight should follow.

Civil war
Fighting that occurs between two sides from the same country.

Coat of arms
A family badge.

Concentric castle
A complicated castle with lots of walls.

Conqueror
Someone who takes over a country.

Continuity
Things staying the same.

Crank
A mechanism that is useful in moving machinery.

Crusades
A series of religious wars between medieval Christianity and medieval Islam. Fought in the Holy Land (the area around Jerusalem).

Early Modern Period
The period of European history which followed the Middle Ages. Lasted from 1450 to 1789.

Elected
Being voted into power by the choice of the people.

Empathy
Looking at a situation from another person's viewpoint.

Fallow
Leaving a field to recover for a year before growing crops on it.

Fealty
A solemn oath of loyalty which is sworn as part of the feudal system.

Feudal system
The power structure between the king, barons, knights and peasants that William the Conqueror introduced to help him run England.

Flagellants
A group of people who whipped themselves in an attempt to avoid catching the plague.

Freeman
A type of peasant who owned some land.

Gears
Simple machine parts as may be found on a bicycle.

Guilds
Town organisations that run trades.

Habit
A monk's outfit (brown, black, white or grey depending on the type of monk) designed to be multi-purpose, cheap to make and to conceal the body.

Heraldry
The study and design of coats of arms.

Hermit
A strongly religious person that lives an isolated, holy life.

Housecarls
King Harold's personal bodyguards.

Keep
The part of a castle which the baron and soldiers lived in. The main building of a castle.

Knights
Another word for cavalry. The term 'knight' in the Middle Ages usually means a person from the upper classes.

Longbow
A powerful bow. The favoured weapon of the English in the Hundred Years War.

Lord of the manor
The most important person in an area. Usually a knight.

Mediæval
Another term for the Middle Ages or Medieval Period.

Monastery
The building where monks lived, worked and prayed (plural = monasteries).

Monarch
A king or a queen.

Motive
The reason for performing an action.

Motte and bailey
A wooden castle on a mound (motte), with a lower, enclosed level (bailey) of houses. These were built by William the Conqueror when he first arrived in England.

Mystic
A religious person, often someone who has religious visions and dreams.

Outlaw
Someone in the Middle Ages who has been declared to be a criminal.

Peasant
An ordinary farm worker. Most people in the Medieval Period were peasants and were at the bottom of the feudal system. Serfs, villeins and freemen are all types of peasant.

Period
A phase in history.

Political history
The history of kings, queens, wars and government.

Popular protest
When ordinary people get together to show that they are not happy about something.

Pottage
A kind of soup eaten by peasants.

Printing
Producing large numbers of books with a machine.

Reeve
A village official who was in charge of farming.

Reign
The period of time during which one king or queen rules.

Revolt
When the ruled turn against their rulers.

Rudder
A mechanism used to steer a ship.

Serf
The lowest kind of peasant. They owned no land and had to ask permission to leave their village.

Siege
When an army surrounds a town or castle and either attacks or starves out the inhabitants.

Social history
The history of ordinary people's lives.

Statute of Labourers
Laws passed to try to control peasants after the plague.

Stirrup
A loop of metal, part of a saddle, that a horse-rider puts their foot in.

Stone of Scone
The Scottish symbol of kingship. The Stone can be seen today in Edinburgh Castle.

Successor
Someone who comes after someone else in a particular role, for example Edward II was Edward I's successor.

Suit of armour
Complicated metal suit designed to protect a knight.

Timeline
A series of events put into historical order.

Tonsure
A medieval monk's hairstyle, usually where the top of the head is shaved to leave a bald semi-sphere.

Turning point
An important historical event that really changes the course of society.

Urban
To do with towns.

Villein
A type of peasant who owned some land.

Water wheel
A mechanism that allows the power of moving streams to be tapped and used, e.g. to grind corn.

Yeoman
A middle-class person in the Middle Ages.

Answers

Timeline tangles p5
Romans – mosaic; Dark Ages – helmet; Middle Ages – barn; Early Modern – musket; Modern – computer

Britain - it's foggy, rainy and cold. Why bother? p7

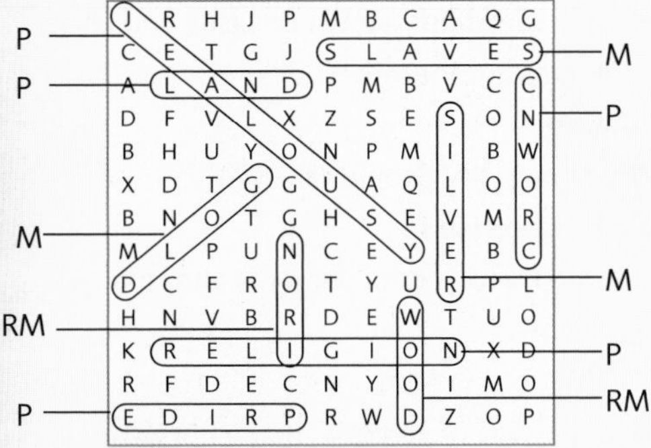

RM, M or P.

If you go down to the woods today p9
1. Aelfric should beware of the wolf, bear, lynx and wild boar.
2. The woolly mammoth is an anachronism.

Hastening to Hastings p13
The correct order of events is: Goes to York, Loses at Fulford, Marches to Hastings, Fights William.

Hastings anagrams p15
The labels on each diagram are as follows.
Harold: helmet, armour
Saxon Housecarl: double-handed axe, shield
Norman Archer: bow, arrow
William: sword
Norman knight: spear, chainmail, helmet, shield

The feudal system - a-maze-ing p17

Castle XXXX p21
The seven anachronisms are: Watch, Ice cream, Lifeguard, Life jacket, Information desk, Ambulance, Machine gun.
The hidden name is WILLIAM.

Attack or defend? p23
The word spells LADDERS.

Domesday difficulties p25
The cunning Saxon farmer has: 30 chickens, 45 sheep, 40 cows, 80 geese, 20 goats.

Church crossword p29
1 Bats 2 Yew 3 Sundial 4 Coffin 5 Porch 6 Graveyard
The hidden word is BELFRY.

A monk's busy day p31
7 AM ~~Carp~~pra~~eel~~y → Pray
8 AM ~~Pike~~chu~~sole~~rch → Church
9 AM Cop~~trout~~y bo~~cod~~ok → Copy book
10 AM Gard~~salmon~~ening → Gardening
11 AM ~~Minnow~~pray~~char~~ → Pray
12 Noon ~~Shark~~chur~~barracuda~~ch → Church
1 PM ~~Perch~~preach~~perch~~ → Preach

Middle English muddle p33
1	Cristen = Christian	14	Understonde = Understand
11	Smylying = Smiling	10	Ttrappe = Trap
3	Oxenford = Oxford	2	Myghte = Might
13	Syde = Side	8	Ooffryng = Offering
9	Frenssh = French	7	Flours = Flowers
6	Iren = Iron	12	Curteis = Courteous
4	Everich = Every	5	Ruste = Rust

The hidden job is CUSTOMS OFFICER.

Sam's stolen stuff p37
Sam's shears, stool and arrows have been stolen.

Streetwise p39

Medieval food puzzle p41
1. Pottage
2. Apple
3. Radish
4. Sweetmeats
5. Lord
6. Evening
7. Yuck

The hidden words are PARSLEY and HERB.

The grail quest p45
Sir Ian finds the grail.

Shield mirror images p47
1B 2C 3B 4A

Agincourt line up p49

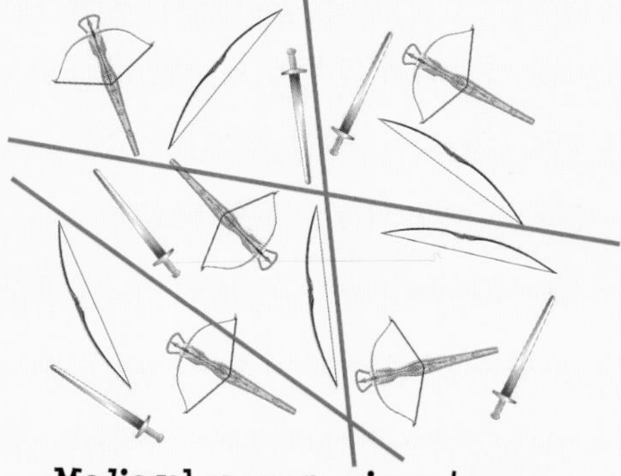

Medieval women mix-up! p53

1	Trotula	Was a medical writer
2	Julian of Norwich	Stayed in one room all of her life
3	Melisende	Ran Jerusalem
4	Eleanor	Lionheart's mum (very powerful)
5	Matilda	Queen of England
6	Joan of Arc	Fought and defeated the English
7	Hildegarde	Wrote music and books

P55

1 Shin hacking
2 Falconry
3 Boar hunting
4 Bear baiting or bull baiting
5 Cock fighting
6 Deer hound
7 Trapball
8 Football

John's text message p57

The message is: Help I have lost my treasure.

Beaumaris castle p61

Scottish crossword p63

Across
1 Spider
2 Balliol
3 Scot
4 Mel
5 Crown

Down
1 Scone
2 Bannockburn
3 William
4 Robert

Roman-Arabic mathematical problems p65

1 24
2 30
3 2006
4 1066
5 1200
6 73
7 272
8 303
9 5439
10 65

Plague - true or false? p69

True: 1, 4, 5, 7
False: 2, 3, 6

Peasants' Revolt wordsearch p71

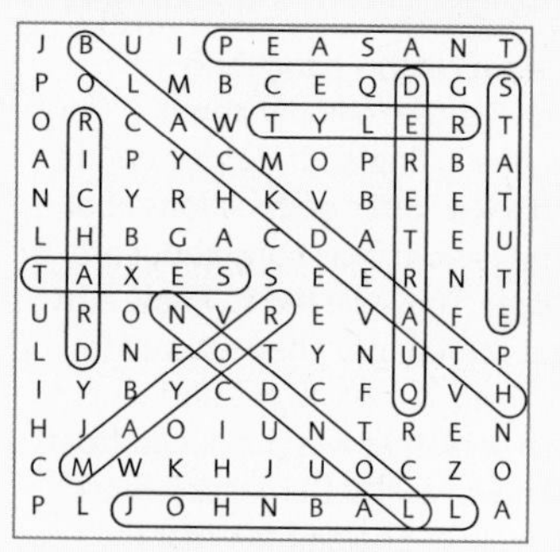

Rose gardening p73

Richard III holds the white rose of the York family.
Henry VII holds the red rose of the Lancaster family.

Test your knowledge 1

1 a) Middle Ages b) The Dark Ages c) Anglo-Saxon d) Early Modern e) Tudor Period f) King Alfred g) Viking h) Roman i) Britannia j) Scandinavia
2 a) AD 43 b) 7th c) 9th d) 849 e) 1066, 1485 f) 1485, 1603 g) 1603, 1714 h) 1714, 1837 i) 1837, 1901 j) 1901, 1910
3 a) Wolf b) Offa's Dyke, The Ridgeway c) Wild boar d) Lynx e) About 1.5 million
4 a) C – Bourbons were not an English royal family.
b) B – Birmingham was not an important Saxon town.
c) A – Chips was not a reason to invade England.
d) D – Khan never came to England.

Test your knowledge 2

1 a) Confessor b) Normandy c) Edgar d) Norway e) Stamford Bridge f) Battle g) Shield h) Housecarls i) Senlac j) King k) Peasants l) Hereward the Wake m) France
2 a) January 1066 b) September 1066 c) September 1066 d) October 1066 e) December 1066
3 a) Cavalry, archers b) He was too young. c) Fulford d) He was killed by an arrow in his eye. e) Barons
4 a) B – Richard I was not involved in the events of 1066.
b) A – Guns were not used at Hastings.
c) B – Bannockburn was not fought in 1066.
d) C – All the others are duties under the feudal system.

Test your knowledge 3

1 a) Motte b) Keep c) Bailey d) Concentric e) Motte and bailey f) Domesday Book g) Barons or knights h) Towns, river crossings, ports, road crossings
2 When a castle is attacked we say it is being *beseiged*. The aim for the defenders is to stay in the castle until help comes. The attackers' aim is to get into the castle or *starve* the inhabitants. The defender hides behind thick walls and fires arrows from *arrow slits*. The defenders can also pour boiling oil or water from *machiolations* onto the attackers below.
The besieger will try to knock down walls and towers with *trebuchets* a type of catapult. Sometimes they even fire dead bodies into the castle to try to poison the occupants. They will also dig tunnels called *saps* to undermine the walls. To go over the walls, a besieger will use *siege towers* or ladders. The invention of the

cannon was an important turning point as they could easily blast the walls.

3 Cross out the wrong words in this paragraph. William the Conqueror wanted to know about *resources available to him* in England. He decided to send out inspectors to ask *a series of questions about villages and towns*. They asked questions about *the area of land in the village*. They wanted to know *how many animals were in each village*. They wanted to find out how many people *lived in the villages* and what *people they were*. The book that was produced from this information was known as the *Domesday Book*. This is because the people of England felt that the questioning was as inescapable as the end of the world.

4 a) C – A bunker is a modern military defence.
b) D – A homing missile is modern.
c) A – Turkeys would not be kept in the Middle Ages.
d) D – You don't need spoons to make a castle.

Test your knowledge 4

1 a) 1300 and 1399 b) 525 c) 1340s
2 a) Hell b) Science c) Health d) Doom paintings
3 a) Tower b) Graveyard c) Tower d) Side of the church e) Holding up the wall f) Roof
4 a) Monastery b) Habits c) Writing and copying books, teaching, advising kings, sheltering travellers, farming, looking after the sick, giving charity, praying for souls, preaching d) Nun e) Tonsure
5 a) C – Epples was not a name for eggs in Chaucer's time.
b) A – Middle English was made up of the other three languages.
c) D – Eating crisps was not done by monks.
d) D – Trainers were not worn by monks.

Test your knowledge 5

1 In a medieval village, the most important person was the *lord* who lived in the manor house. His official, the steward, would tell the *reeve* what to do, and he in turn would tell the villagers. There were different types of villagers. The *serfs* were the lowest of the low and they often owned no *land*. Just above them were *villeins* and *freemen*. These villagers are known collectively as *peasants*.

2 In the Middle Ages, towns usually had a *charter*. This was *a legal document* that outlined the town's rights. Usually *a mayor* ran a town. He would usually have been *elected*. The powerful organisations within the town would have been the various *guilds*. These ran all of the *trades*.
A medieval town would have had lots of *rubbish* in the street. It was easy to catch *diseases* and they were not hygienic places to live. However, a townsman would have more *freedom* than a villager.

3 a) Potato b) Wine c) A type of soup d) Rough e) Beer
4 a) C – Turkeys come from America.
b) A – Peasants didn't have dishwashers.
c) D – Medieval towns didn't have bowling alleys.
d) B – A lord was upper class, the others are peasants.
e) C – You would never find sweetcorn in a Medieval field.

Test your knowledge 6

1 a) Edward III b) Crecy c) Poitiers d) Agincourt e) Charles VI f) Joan of Arc g) King Arthur h) Round i) William Shakespeare j) Order of the Garter
2 a) 1340, 1460 b) 1346 c) 1356 d) 1415 e) 1422 f) 400 g) 26 h) 1189–1199
3 a) Supporters b) The motto c) Horse, coat, banner, shield d) Heraldry e) Three lions
4 a) C – The correct heraldic term is mantling not mantlepiece.
b) C – Richard I was not involved in the Hundred Years War.
c) A – Hastings was not a battle in the Hundred Years War.
d) B – Machine guns were not used in the Hundred Years War.
e) B – Knee flaps are not part of a suit of armour.

Test your knowledge 7

1 a) 55 b) Trotula of Salerno, Hildegard c) 1179 d) Joan of Arc e) Queen Matilda f) 1416 g) 82
2 King John has not got a good reputation. Two of his nicknames are *Lackland* and *Softsword*. This is because he lost battles and much of England's lands in France. Magna Carta is *Latin* and means *Great Charter*. It was signed by King John in *1215*. It was the *barons* who made him sign. The Magna Carta was an important step in the development of English politics. King John is also known for losing his treasure in an *estuary*.
3 a) The Sheriff of Nottingham b) A myth or legend c) Outlaws d) The forest laws e) King John
4 a) False b) True c) True d) True e) True f) False g) False h) False i) False j) False

Test your knowledge 8

1 a) Edward I b) James of St George c) Longshanks, Hammer of the Scots d) The Prince of Wales e) Offa's Dyke f) Great g) Strong, weak, strong h) Stone of Scone i) Balliol j) Bannockburn
2 a) 1307 b) 1327 c) 1096 d) 1267 e) 1284 f) 1286 g) 1603 h) 1377 i) 1067 j) 400
3 a) Roman numerals b) Christianity and Islam c) Richard I (Lionheart) d) Chess e) Algebra
4 a) B – P is not a Roman numeral.
b) D – Edam cheese was not introduced as a result of the Crusades.
c) D – Mel Gibson was not a real ruler of Scotland.
d) C – The Playstation was not invented in the Middle Ages.
e) A – The Millennium Stadium is a Welsh landmark but not one of Edward's castles.

Test your knowledge 9

1 17
2 Henry III
3 Richard III
4 4
5 2
6 Plantagenets
7 York
8 William II, Edward II, Richard II, Henry VI
9 Overeating
10 I love them all!